$2

MEMORIES AND COMMENTARIES

1. Myself and Robert Craft at Paestum, 1959

MEMORIES
AND
COMMENTARIES

IGOR STRAVINSKY

and

ROBERT CRAFT

FABER AND FABER

24 Russell Square

London

First published in mcmlx
by Faber and Faber Limited
24 Russell Square London W.C.1
Printed in Great Britain by
Latimer Trend & Co Ltd Plymouth

To
NADIA BOULANGER

Socrates, to the Eleatic Stranger: '. . . I shall
only beg of you to say whether you like and
are accustomed to make a long oration on a
subject which you want to explain to another
. . . or to proceed by the method of question and
answer. I remember hearing a very noble discussion in which Parmenides employed the
latter of the two methods, when I was a young
man, and he was far advanced in years.'

—SOPHIST 217

CONTENTS

AUTOBIOGRAPHICAL

    1. A Russian Education   *page* 17

    2. Diaghilev and his Dancers   31

    3. Some Russian Composers   54
        Rimsky-Korsakov   54
        Cui   60
        Arensky   61
        Taneyev   62
        Liadov   62
        Scriabin   64
        Prokofiev   66

PORTRAITS MÉMOIRES
        Valéry   73
        Rolland   78
        Falla   80
        Hahn   81
        Gorodetsky and Balmont   82
        Berners   83
        Royauté   85

SOME MUSICAL QUESTIONS   91

Contents

THREE OPERAS

    1. *The Nightingale* (letters from Alexander Benois)   *page* 131

    2. *Persephone* (letters from André Gide)   144

    3. *The Rake's Progress* (letters from W. H. Auden)   154

APPENDIX—First Scenario for *The Rake's Progress*   167

    INDEX   177

ILLUSTRATIONS

1. Myself and Robert Craft at Paestum, 1959. *frontispiece*

2. Myself in 1886. *facing page* 20

3. Four brothers, in 1893. 21

4. My mother and father, *c.* 1900, in our house in St. Petersburg. 28

5. Monte Carlo, in front of the Riviera Palace Hotel, 16th April 1911. 29

6. On the balcony of Ravel's apartment, avenue Carnot, Paris, 1911. The sisters Botkin, P. Koribut-Kubitovitch (a cousin of Diaghilev's), Karsavina, Nijinsky, myself, Benois, Diaghilev and Mme Bezobrazov. 32

7. At Beau Soleil (above Monte Carlo), 1911. 33

8. With Diaghilev and the Russian General, Bezobrazov, at Beau Soleil, 1911. 33

9. Nijinsky, Isola Bella, June, 1912. 48

10. Myself, *ibidem*, looking like a Bersagliere. 48

11. With Ravel, Clarens, 1913. 49

12. Ravel, Nijinsky, Bronislava Nijinska, 1913. 64

13. A page of my Tsarist passport. 65

14. Sketch for the cover of my *Ragtime* by Picasso, 1919. 80

15. Sketch for the cover of my *Ragtime* by Picasso, 1919. 81

13

Illustrations

16. Diaghilev, drawn by me, 1921. *facing page* 96
17. Bakst, drawn by me, 1921. 96
18. Madrid, 1921. Robert Delaunay, Boris Kochno, myself, Sonia Delaunay, Diaghilev, Manuel de Falla, Barocchi (the first husband of Lopokova). 97
19. Cocteau, Picasso, myself, Olga Picasso, Antibes, 1926. 112
20. Myself, Prokofiev, Pierre Souvtchinsky, at Talloires (Lac d'Annecy), 1929. 113
21. With Gide in Wiesbaden, 1933. 144
22. With Charles Chaplin, Hollywood, 1937. Photograph by King Vidor, courtesy of *Life Magazine*. 145

AUTOBIOGRAPHICAL

GENEALOGICAL TABLE

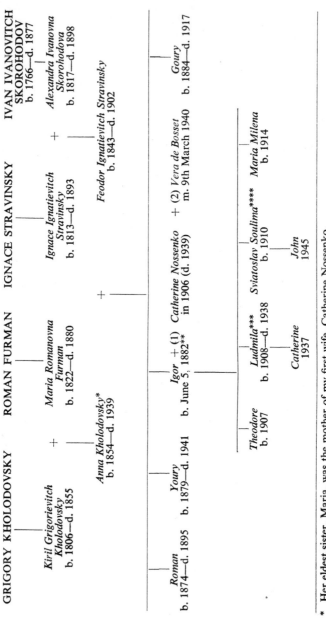

* Her eldest sister, Maria, was the mother of my first wife, Catherine Nossenko.
** Old Style. My birthday is 17th June 1882, New Style, but because the difference between the Gregorian and Julian calendars increases by one day each century, it has been 18th June since 1900. In only 23,360 centuries I shall have been born later than my grandson.
*** Married Youry Mandelstam who was killed by the Germans in Poland sometime between 1941 and 1945.
**** Married Françoise Blondlat.

1

A RUSSIAN EDUCATION

FAMILY

.C. Do you know the origin of your name?

S. 'Stravinsky' comes from 'Strava', the name of a small river, tributary to the Vistula, in eastern Poland. We were originally called Soulima-Stravinsky—Soulima being the name of another Vistula branch—but when Russia annexed this part of Poland the Soulima was for some reason dropped. The Soulima-Stravinskys were landowners in eastern Poland, as far back as they can be traced. In the reign of Catherine the Great they moved from Poland to Russia.

.C. Would you draw your family tree?

S. (See chart.)

.C. What do you know about your grandparents and great-grandparents?

S. The only great-grandparent about whom I had heard anything at all was Roman Furman, and about him I know only that he was a high 'Excellency', that he came from the Baltic provinces, and that he was also an ancestor of Diaghilev's—which made Diaghilev my distant cousin. Of my grandfathers, too, I know very little. Ignace Stravinsky was more famous for his escapades with women than for anything else, and stories of his Don Juan-like behaviour reached me in my childhood. His amorous propensities continued until his very old age and were an embarrassment to my very staid father. He was a Pole, and therefore a Catholic, but Alexandra Skorohodova was Orthodox; according to Russian law the children of a mixed marriage had to be Orthodox, so my father was baptized in the Russian Church. Rimsky used to tease me, saying: 'So your grandfather's name was Ignace? I smell a Catholic there.' Kiril Kholodovsky was born in Kiev, a 'little Russian', as the Kievlani are called. He was a minister of agriculture and served on the Tsar's famous 'Council of Thirty'. He died of tuberculosis, a disease that has attacked our family ever since: my wife, Catherine Nossenko, her mother (who was my aunt), and our elder daughter died of it; my younger daughter and granddaughter have spent years in sanatoriums with it, and I myself have suffered from it at various times, but most severely in 1939 when I was five months in the sanatorium at Sancellemoz.

R.C. And about your parents?

I.S. I only know that they met in my mother's city of Kiev, where my father was the first basso of the Opera, and that they were married there. My father had been a law student in the Niéjinsky Lyceum when he discovered his good bass voice and good musical ear. He went from the Lyceum to the St. Petersburg Conservatory and became a pupil of Professor Everardi, whose school for the voice was as celebrated as Auer's school for the violin. At graduation he accepted a position in the Kiev Opera which he held for a few years until he was ready for the Opera in St. Petersburg.

R.C. Did anyone in your family beside your father possess musical ability?

I.S. I think not. At least I never heard my father or mother claim any musical talent for their parents or grandparents, and I know that my father considered his own musical ear and memory as a kind of supra-Mendelian phenomenon. I should add, however, that my mother was a competent pianist and a good sight-reader, and that she was at least mildly interested in music all her life.

R.C. How did it happen that you were born in Oranienbaum— that is, why did your family move there from St. Petersburg?

S. Oranienbaum was a pleasant seaside village built round an eighteenth-century palace. It faced Kronstadt, and my parents had gone there a month before I was born to enjoy the early summer air. We never returned to Oranienbaum after my birth, however, and I have never seen it since—if I saw it then. My friend Charles-Albert Cingria—a critic of 'the Stravinsky of the international style'—used to call me 'le maître d'Oranienbaum'.

R.C. Can you describe your father's character?

S. Oh, oh, he was not very *commode*. In fact, I was constantly frightened of him, which, I suppose, has deeply harmed my own character. He had an uncontrollable temper, and life with him was very difficult. He would lose himself in his anger, suddenly and unexpectedly, and without regard to where he might happen to be. I remember being terribly humiliated in a street in Bad Homburg when he suddenly ordered me to return to our hotel room—I was in my eleventh or twelfth year—and when I sulked instead of immediately obeying him, he caused a major scandal in the street. He was affectionate to me only when I was ill—which seems to me an excellent excuse for any hypochondriac tendencies I might have. Whether or not to gain his affection, I caught pleurisy when I was thirteen and was left with tuberculosis for a time afterwards. During this period of illness he was a different man to me and I forgave him everything that had happened before. He was a distant parent, however—distant not only to his children but also, or so he seemed to me, to his surroundings. He impressed me in his death more than he had ever

19

done in his life. He had once fallen on the stage of the Opera
and, some time later, he suddenly complained of great pain in
his back in the place that had been struck by the fall. He went
to Berlin for Röntgen treatment, but the cancer, which is
what it was, had developed beyond hope of cure. He died a
year and a half later, on the couch in his study, saying, 'I feel
so good, so very good.' His death brought us close together.

R.C. And the character of your mother and brothers?

I.S. I was close to no one in my family except my brother Goury.
For my mother I felt only 'duties'. My feelings were all fixed
upon Bertha, my nurse. Bertha was an East Prussian who
knew almost no Russian; German was the language of my
nursery. Perhaps I should blame Bertha for corrupting me
(somewhat as Byron must have been corrupted in Aberdeen
by May Gray), but I do not. She lived on to nurse my own
children and was forty years in our family when she died, in
Morges, in 1917. I mourned her more than I did, later, my
mother. When I remember my older brothers at all, it is to
remind myself how exceedingly they used to annoy me.
Roman was a law student. At eleven he caught diphtheria
which weakened his heart and killed him ten years later. I
thought him a very handsome brother and I was proud of
him, but I could not confide in him for he was absolutely
untouched by music.

Youry—George—was an architectural engineer and he
continued to work as one in Leningrad until his death there in
1941. He was not close to me as a child, nor later, for he never
wrote to me when I left Russia, and I last saw him in 1908.
His wife did write to me once in Paris, however, and in 1925
their elder daughter Tatiana visited me there. Youry died
shortly before the German invasion, as I learned from a Mr.
Borodin, a friend of Rimsky's eldest son Michael, who used
to send me letters from somewhere on Long Island with news
of friends of mine in Russia; I heard of Andrei Rimsky-

2. Myself in 1886

Roman

Youry

Igor

Goury

3. Four brothers, in 1893

Korsakov's death from him (but I also had this news from Rachmaninov), of Maximilian Steinberg's, and finally of Youry's.

Goury began his career, like Roman and myself, as a law student. He had inherited my father's voice and musical ear, however, and he was determined to be a singer. Rather than enter the Conservatory he studied with Tartakov, a famous St. Petersburg singer, and sang professionally in a private St. Petersburg theatre from 1912–14. To my great regret I did not hear him there, but Diaghilev did, and reported to me that Goury was very good. He had a baritone voice, like my father's in quality, but not so low. I composed my Verlaine songs for him and I was always grieved that he did not live to sing them professionally. He was conscripted early in the 1914 war and sent to the southern front in a Red Cross unit. He died of scarlet fever in Rumania, in April 1917, and was buried next to my father in St. Petersburg's Alexandro-Nevsky cemetery, which the Bolsheviks later turned into a national artists' cemetery. Goury and my father were both respected by the Bolsheviks—a glorification that seems very remote now. My father had been buried in the Novodevitchy (the New Maiden) cemetery, but was re-buried in the Alexandro-Nevsky cemetery in 1917, with Tchaikovsky, Rimsky, Dostoievsky, Gogol, and, I think, Leskov.

Though I had not seen Goury since 1910, his death made me very lonely. We had been together constantly as children, and we felt that as long as we *were* together, all was well with the world. We found in each other the love and under-standing denied us by our parents, who specially favoured neither of us, though Goury was in some respects the Ben-jamin of the family.

R.C. Did your parents recognize your musical talent?

S.　No. The only member of the family who believed I had any

was my uncle Alexander Ielatchitch. I think that my father judged my possibilities as a musician from his own experience and decided that the musical life would be too difficult for me. I could hardly blame him, however, for before his death I had written nothing, and though I was progressing in my piano technique it was already clear that I would not become a virtuoso of that instrument.

Alexander Ielatchitch had married my mother's sister Sophie five years before my father's marriage. His five children were therefore just enough older than the four of us to ensure that we suffered an ample amount of taunting and misery. I still resent the way they despised us because of their superior age, and I am even now a little triumphant that I have outlived them all. But Uncle Ielatchitch himself was nice to me. He owned vast farms and forests in the Samara Government, east of the Volga, where he invited us to spend our summers with him. I composed my first large-scale work there, incidentally, the lost—fortunately lost—piano sonata.

The four-day trips on the Volga to Pavlovka, as the Ielatchitch Samara estate was called, were among the happiest days of my life. I first made the trip in 1885 (*sic*), but of that I remember only a portrait of the Tsar on the wall of our state-room (which was supposed to have made me cry 'conductor', for his cap and uniform were like those of a railway conductor). The second excursion came eighteen years later, and my companion this time was Vladimir Rimsky-Korsakov. We heralded his father with postcards from each of the boat's stopping places: Rybinsk (literally, 'fish-town'), a white and gold city with monasteries and glittering churches—it looked like a set of *Tsar Saltan,* as one came upon it round a sudden bend in the river; Jaroslav, with its blue and gold churches and its yellow, Italian-style office buildings (I saw coloured slides of Jaroslav recently in Manila, at Ambassador Bohlen's); and Nishni-Novgorod where, surrounded by mendicant monks, we would walk to little booths where we bought and drank kumiss (mare's milk).

Uncle Ielatchitch who, as I have said in our first book, introduced me to the music of Brahms, adored Beethoven and was, I think, a good guide in my early understanding of that composer. He had two portraits on the wall of his study, Renan—Uncle Ielatchitch was a liberal—and Beethoven. The latter was a copy of the Waldmüller portrait. It seemed to contradict the whole hero-worshipping notion of Beethoven then prevalent. (In fact, as a small child I did not know it was Beethoven until one day while playing in the sand-dunes of the Alexander Park I saw an old woman whose face was exactly the face on my uncle's wall, which led me to ask my uncle who the woman was.) In any case, I did not hero-worship Beethoven, nor have I ever done so, and the nature of Beethoven's talent and work are more 'human' and more comprehensible to me than are, say, the talents and works of more 'perfect' composers like Bach and Mozart; I think I know how Beethoven composed.[1] I have little enough Beethoven in me, alas, but some people have found I have some. Someone has even compared the first movement of the *Eroica*, bars 272–5, with the three chords following Fig. 173 in *Le Sacre*, with Fig. 22 in *Renard*, and with the same musical figure in the first movement of my *Symphony in Three Movements*, bars 69–71.

R.C. Would you describe your home in St. Petersburg?

---

[1] Though I do not understand how a man of such powers could lapse so frequently into such banality. The octave passage for violins in the *Malinconia* (op. 18, no. 6) is an early and tiny example of what I mean. A late and terrible example is the first movement of the ninth symphony. How could Beethoven have been satisfied—if he was satisfied—with such quadrilateral phrasing and pedantic development (cf. bars 387-400), such poor rhythmic invention (how

dull is), and such patently false pathos.

The mere fact that I can talk about Beethoven in this fashion proves my point, however, for about Bach I can only say that he is so elegant, so wise, so 'indispensable'.

I.S. We occupied a flat in a large old house: apartment 66, Krukov Canal. The house no longer exists, thanks to a German bomb, but Ansermet could give a description of it more recent than my own, for he visited my brother there in 1938. It was a four-storey house. We lived on the third floor, and, at one time, Karsavina rented the floor above us. On the other side of the canal stood a very handsome empire-style building, yellow in colour like the Villa Medici in Rome— but a prison, unfortunately. The building next to us was an apartment house also, and the conductor Napravnik lived there.

Our flat was furnished in the usual Victorian manner— with the usual bad paintings, the usual mauve upholstery, etc., but with an unusual library and two grand pianos. To recall it gives me no pleasure, however. I do not like to remember my childhood, and the four walls of my and Goury's room represent my most abiding impression of home. Our room was like Petroushka's cell, and most of my time was spent there. I was allowed out of doors only after my parents had put me through a medical examination, and I was considered too frail to participate in any sports or games when I *was* out. I suspect even now that my hatred of sports is my jealousy at having been deprived of them.

A new life began for me after the death of my father, when I began to live more in accordance with my own wishes. I even left home altogether on one occasion, leaving my mother the traditional note to the effect that life at 66 Krukov Canal was impossible. I sought refuge with a recently married Ielatchitch cousin, a man devoted to any form of revolution or protestation, but after a few days my mother managed to fall ill enough to force me to come back. She did behave slightly less egotistically after that, however, and her delight in torturing me seemed slightly less intense. I continued to live at home during the first year of my marriage, then moved to another apartment on the English Prospect, my last residence in St. Petersburg.

TEACHERS

R.C. Would you describe your piano lessons with Mlle Kashperova?

I.S. She was an excellent pianist and a blockhead—a not unusual combination. By which I mean that her aesthetics and her bad taste were impregnable but her pianism of a high order. She was well known in St. Petersburg, and though her name would not appear in Grove or Riemann, I think she might have been listed in a Russian dictionary of the time. She talked endlessly about her teacher, Anton Rubinstein, and I was attentive to this because I had seen Rubinstein in his coffin. (It was a sight I shall never forget. I was somewhat prepared for it because at an even earlier age I had seen the dead Emperor Alexander III—a yellow, waxen, uniformed doll— lying in State in the S.S. Peter and Paul Cathedral. Rubinstein was white, but with a thick black mane; he was in full dress, as though for a concert, and his hands were folded over a Cross; I did not see Tchaikovsky in his coffin, incidentally, because my parents thought the weather too dangerously bad for me to risk going out.) I learned to play the Mendelssohn G minor concerto with Mlle Kashperova, and many sonatas by Clementi and Mozart, as well as sonatas and other pieces by Haydn, Beethoven, Schubert and Schumann. Chopin was forbidden, and she tried to discourage my interest in Wagner. Nevertheless, I knew all Wagner's works from the piano scores, and when I was sixteen or seventeen, and at last had the money to buy them, from the orchestral scores. We played Rimsky's operas together four-hands, and I remember deriving much pleasure from *Christmas Eve* this way. Mlle Kashperova's only idiosyncrasy as a teacher was in forbidding me all use of pedals; I had to sustain with my fingers, like an organist—an omen, perhaps, as I have never been a pedal composer. I am most in Kashperova's debt, however, for something she would not have appreciated. Her narrowness and her formulae greatly encouraged the supply of bitterness that accumulated in my soul until, in my mid-twenties, I broke loose and revolted from her and from every stultification in my studies, my schools, and my family. The real answer to your questions about my childhood is that it was a period of waiting for the moment when I could send everyone and everything connected with it to hell.

R.C. What schools did you attend in St. Petersburg?

I.S. I attended a government school, the Second St. Petersburg Gymnasium, until I was fourteen or fifteen. From there I went to the Gourévitch Gymnasium, a private school where Youry had been before me. The Gourévitch Gymnasium was about eight miles from our house, in a neighbourhood called 'peski', 'the sands', and these eight miles kept me in constant debt. Always too late in the mornings for the tram, I would have to take a fiacre and pay forty or fifty kopecks. But the fiacre rides were the only thing about school I liked, especially in winter. On the way home, what a pleasure it was to drive through the Nevsky Prospect in a sleigh, protected by a net from the dirty snow kicked up by the horse, and then, at home, to warm myself in front of our big white porcelain stove.

The Gourévitch Gymnasium was divided into a 'classical' and a *Realschule*. My own curriculum belonged to the former: history, Latin, Greek, Russian and French literatures, mathematics. I was of course a very bad pupil, and I hated this school as I did all my schools, profoundly and forever.

R.C. Did you have any sympathetic teachers?

I.S. My mathematics professor in this same Gourévitch Gymnasium—a man called Woolf—did understand me, I think. He was an ex-Hussar officer with a real talent for mathematics, but he had been, and still was, a drunkard. (Another of my professors was a drunkard too, a man in perpetual disgrace who would walk to the window, turn his back to us, and steal a nip from a little bottle in his coat pocket; the other boys mocked him cruelly.) Professor Woolf was also an amateur musician. He knew that I composed—I had already been reproached for it by the school director—and he helped, protected, and encouraged me.

UNIVERSITY

R.C. What are your memories of St. Petersburg University?

I.S. As attendance at lectures was optional, I opted not to attend, and in all my four years there I probably did not hear more than fifty. I have only a vague and uninterested memory of the University. I read criminal law and legal philosophy, and I was interested in the theoretical and abstract questions of both, but by the time I entered the University so much of my time was spent with Rimsky-Korsakov I could hardly do justice to any other studies. I can now recall only two incidents connected with my life there. I was walking through the Kazansky Place one afternoon in the politically tense months following the Russo-Japanese war, when a group of students began to stage a protest. The police were prepared, however, and the protestants were arrested, myself with them. I was detained seven hours, but seventy years will not erase the memory of my fears. The other incident occurred during the last spring cramming season, when, realizing that I would never pass one of my examinations, I proposed to exchange names with Nicolai Yussupov, that he might take my examination and I one of his: we were better in each other's subject. Our ruse was never detected because our faces were quite unknown to the professors, but poor Nicolai—whose brother later killed Rasputin—died shortly after passing my paper, in a duel in Tashkent.

R.C. What did you read in your University years?

I.S. Russian literature mostly, and the literature of other countries in Russian translation. Dostoievsky was always my hero. Of the new writers, I liked Gorky most and disliked most Andreyev. The Scandinavians then so popular—Lagerlöf and Hamsun—did not appeal to me at all, but I admired Strindberg and, of course, Ibsen. Ibsen's plays were as popular in Russia in those years as Tchaikovsky's music. Südermann and Hauptmann were also in great vogue then, and Dickens, and Mark Twain (whose daughter I later knew in Hollywood), and Scott, whose *Ivanhoe* (pronounced in Russian as a four-syllable paroxytone—*Ivanhoé*) was as popular a children's book as it ever was in the English-speaking countries.

CONCERTS IN ST. PETERSBURG

R.C. You often mention the St. Petersburg concert series 'Evenings of Contemporary Music'. What music did you hear there?

I.S. First of all, my own. Nicolas Richter played my early piano sonata there, and this was the first music of mine to be performed in public. It was, I suppose, an inept imitation of late Beethoven. I myself performed there, too, as accompanist to a singer, a certain Miss Petrenko, in my Gorodetsky songs. Works by young Russian composers were in the majority, of course, but French music—the quartets and songs of Debussy and Ravel, and various pieces by Dukas and d'Indy—was also promoted.[1] Brahms was played, too, and Reger. Like

[1] When I met d'Indy at a rehearsal of *Le Sacre* in 1921 I told him I had heard an amount of his music in St. Petersburg in my youth, but he probably understood that it had been part of the background that had provoked me into writing *Le Sacre*, for he said nothing.

4. My mother and father, *c.* 1900, in our house in St. Petersburg
   My first knowledge of music was acquired at this piano

5. Monte Carlo, in front of the Riviera Palace Hotel, 16th April 1911. The ladies
dark suits are the sisters Botkin, nieces of the Tsar's doctor. Then, from left to rig
standing, are P. Koribut-Kubitovitch (a cousin of Diaghilev's), Karsavina, Nijins
myself, Benois, Diaghilev. The woman in the foreground is Mme Bezobrazov

Autobiographical

the 'Monday Evening Concerts' in Los Angeles, these St. Petersburg concerts, in spite of their name, tried to match the new with the old. This was important, and rare, for so many organizations are dedicated to new music, and so few to the centuries before Bach. I heard Monteverdi there for the first time, in an arrangement by d'Indy, I think, and Couperin and Montéclair; and Bach was performed in quantity.

The people I met at these concerts were also a great part of the interest. All the composers, the poets, and the artists of St. Petersburg were there, and also the intelligent amateurs— like my friends Ivan Pokrovsky and Stepan Mitusov, who were always aware of the newest art developments in Berlin and Paris.

R.C. Were there any 'advanced' orchestral concerts in St. Petersburg?

I.S. No, the programmes of the Imperial Symphony were very much like the programmes of American orchestras today: standard repertory, and from time to time a piece of second-rate, locally-composed music. The symphonies of Bruckner and Brahms were considered new music still and therefore were rarely and very timidly played. Belayev's 'Russian Symphony Concerts' were more interesting, but they concentrated too much on the Russian 'Five'. Incidentally, I knew Belayev and I met him at concerts. He was the great music patron of his time—a kind of Russian Rockefeller who played the violin. His Editions Belayev in Leipzig had published my *Faune et Bergère*—probably on Rimsky's advice, since Glazunov, his other adviser, would not have recommended it.[1] Once I saw him stand up in his box—he was a tall man with very artistic hair—and stare with amazement at

[1] I am not being unfair to Glazunov; he was so consumed with animosity that when I saw him for the last time, backstage after a concert he conducted in Paris in 1935, and said 'Greetings to you, Alexander Konstantinovitch', all he could do was to look dour, half offer his hand, and say nothing.

the stage where Kussevitsky had just come on carrying his double-bass to play a solo. Belayev turned to me and said: 'Until now such things have been seen only in circuses.'

*   *   *

R.C. What did you love most in Russia?

I.S. The violent Russian spring that seemed to begin in an hour and was like the whole earth cracking. That was the most wonderful event of every year of my childhood.

2

DIAGHILEV AND HIS DANCERS

.C. Do you remember your first attendance at a ballet performance?

S. At the age of seven or eight I was taken to see *The Sleeping Beauty*. I realize now that I was older than this when I saw *A Life for the Tsar*, which contradicts what I said in our first series of conversations, that the latter was my first attendance at a theatrical-musical performance. I was enchanted by the ballet, but I had been prepared for what I saw, for ballet was an important part of our culture and a familiar subject to me from my earliest childhood. Therefore I was able to identify the dance positions and steps, and I knew the plot and the music long in advance. Moreover, Petipa, the choreographer, was a friend of my father's, and I had seen him several times myself. Of the performance itself, I remember only my musical impressions, however, and perhaps those are really my parents' impressions of my impressions, repeated to me afterwards. But I do know that I was excited by the dance and that I applauded it with all my strength. If I could transport myself back to that night seventy years ago I would do so only to satisfy my curiosity about the musical tempi, for I am always interested in the question of tempo in other periods.

Autobiographical

As I grew up I became aware that the ballet was petrifying, that it was, in fact, already quite rigidly conventional. I could not regard it as an exploitable musical medium, of course, and I would have been quite incredulous had anyone suggested that a modern movement in the arts was to be born through it. But would that movement have taken place without Diaghilev? I do not think so.

PAVLOVA

R.C. What ballet dancer did you most admire in your student years?

I.S. Anna Pavlova. She was never a member of Diaghilev's company, however, though Diaghilev had very much wanted her to join. I met her in December 1909 at her home in St. Petersburg. Diaghilev had asked her to invite me to a party, hoping that after she had met me she might agree to dance the part of the Firebird. I remember that Benois and Fokine were there that night, too, and that we drank much champagne. But whatever Pavlova thought of me personally, she did not dance in the *Firebird*. The reasons for her refusal were, I think, my *Scherzo Fantastique* and *Fireworks*. She considered these pieces horribly decadent. ('Decadent' and 'modern' were interchangeable then, whereas 'decadent' now very often means 'not modern enough'.)

The lines of Pavlova's form and her mobile expression were ever beautiful to behold, but the dance itself was always the same and quite devoid of constructive interest. In fact, I remember no difference in her dance from the first time I saw it, in St. Petersburg in 1905 or 1906, to the last time, which was in Paris in the 1930s. Pavlova was an *artiste*, but of an art far removed from the world of the Diaghilev Ballet.

R.C. Who taught you most about the technique of the dance?

6. On the balcony of Ravel's apartment, avenue Carnot, Paris, 1911
The photo is by Ravel

7. At Beau Soleil (above Monte Carlo), 1911

8. With Diaghilev and the Russian General, Bezobrazov, at Beau Soleil, 1911

S. Maestro Cecchetti, the elder of the Ballet and the final authority for every dance step in every ballet we did. Everyone in the company from Nijinsky to the apprentices venerated him. He was a very cosy man and I had become friends with him already in St. Petersburg. His knowledge was limited to the classical dance, of course, and he therefore opposed the trend of our Ballet as a whole, but it was precisely his academicism, not his aesthetics, that Diaghilev required. He remained the Company's dance-conscience throughout its entire existence. There was a Signora Cecchetti too, also a dancer, and as like her husband as a twin. Diaghilev called her 'the Cecchetti in petticoats'. I once saw her dance in crinolines and with a great papier mâché boat on her head. Imagine how delighted I was when Cecchetti agreed to dance the Magician in *Petroushka*. We didn't have to paste a false beard on *him*!

FOKINE

R.C. Do you remember Fokine's choreography for the original *Firebird* and *Petroushka*?

S. I do, but I didn't really like the dance movement of either ballet. The female dancers in the *Firebird*, the Princesses, were insipidly sweet, while the male dancers were the *ne plus ultra* of brute masculinity: in the Kastchei scene, they sat on the floor kicking their legs in an incredibly stupid manner. I prefer Balanchine's choreography for the 1945 version of the *Firebird* suite to the whole Fokine ballet (and the music too: the music of the complete ballet is too long and patchy in quality).

Nor did Fokine realize my ideas for *Petroushka*, though I suspect that this time the fault was rather with Diaghilev than with Fokine. I conceived the Charlatan as a character out of Hoffman, a lackey in a tightly modelled blue *frac*

C

33

with gold stars, and not at all as a Russian Metropolitan. The flute music, too, is Weber-like, or Hoffmann-like, not Russian 'Five'. Also, I had thought of the Moor as a kind of Wilhelm Busch caricature and not as the merely mechanical comic-relief character he is usually made out to be. Another of my ideas was that Petroushka should watch the dances of the Fourth Tableau (the Coachmen, the Nurses, etc.) from a hole in his cell and that we, the audience, should see them, too, from the perspective of his cell. I never did like the full-stage dance carrousel at this point of the drama. And Fokine's choreography was ambiguous at the most important moment. Petroushka's ghost, as I conceived the story, is the real Petroushka, and his appearance at the end makes the Petroushka of the preceding play a mere doll. His gesture is not one of triumph or protest, as is so often said, but a nose-thumbing addressed to the audience. The significance of this gesture is not and never was clear in Fokine's staging. One great invention of Fokine's, however, was the rigid arm movement that Nijinsky was to make such an unforgettable gesture.

Fokine was easily the most disagreeable man I have ever worked with. In fact, with Glazunov, he was the most dis-agreeable man I have ever met; but Glazunov was a time-to-time drunkard which redeemed him—from time to time; he would lock his door for two-week binges on Château Yquem! Imagine bingeing on Château Yquem! I was never a friend of Fokine's, not even in our first years together, for I was a partisan of Cecchetti's, and Cecchetti was for him the merest academician. Diaghilev agreed with me, however, that his dances for *Prince Igor* suggested that he was the best qualified of our choreographers to deal with the *Firebird*. Then, after the *Firebird* and *Petroushka*, I had little to do with him. He was spoiled by his success in America and ever after wore the 'I-have-made-an-American-kill' look. I saw him last with Ida

Rubinstein. He was to have choreographed my *Baiser de la Fée* for her but finally Bronislava Nijinska did it, and I was much relieved. After that and until the end of his life (1940) I received complaints from him about business or royalty matters connected with the *Firebird*, which he would actually refer to as *my* 'musical accompaniment' to *his* 'choreographic poem'.

NIJINSKY AND NIJINSKA

.C. Have you any further recollections to add to what you have already written about Vaslav Nijinsky?

.S. When Diaghilev introduced me to Nijinsky—it was in St. Petersburg in 1909—I was aware of him as an extraordinary physical being. I was aware, too, of curious absences in his personality. I liked his shy manner and his soft, Polish speech, and he was immediately very open and affectionate with me—but he was always that. Later, when I knew him better, I thought him childishly spoiled and impulsive. Later, too, I came to understand the absences as a kind of stigmata; I could not imagine that they would so soon and so tragically destroy him. I often think of Nijinsky in his final years, a captive in his own mind, his most perfect gift of expression in movement stricken, immobile.

*　　　　　*　　　　　*

Already a celebrity when I first knew him, Nijinsky was to become even more celebrated shortly afterwards because of a scandal. Diaghilev had taken charge of his costuming—they were living together—with the result that Nijinsky appeared at the Imperial Theatre in the tightest tights anyone had ever seen (in fact, an athletic support padded with handkerchiefs), and little else. The Tsar's mother had attended a performance and was shocked. Diaghilev and Prince Wolkonsky, the

Director of the Theatre and a man of similar sensibilities, were thought to have conspired against public decency. The Tsar himself was shocked. He alluded to the matter in conversation with Diaghilev but was so curtly answered that Diaghilev was never thereafter in official good odour. I discovered this for myself when Diaghilev asked me to approach Ambassador Izvolsky in an attempt to secure a passport for a dancer of conscription age. When Izvolsky understood my request to be on Diaghilev's behalf he became quite coldly diplomatic. (But I was often Diaghilev's ambassador in later years, especially his 'financial' ambassador—or, as he called me, his tax-collector.)

To return to the Imperial Theatre scandal, the truth is that the exhibitionist was not Nijinsky but Diaghilev. Nijinsky was always very serious and high-minded and, in my judgment, never conscious of his performances from Diaghilev's point of view. I was even more certain of this later, in Paris, when he danced the *Afternoon of a Faun*. This ballet's famous representation of the act of love, and its exhibition of sexual organs, was entirely Diaghilev's idea. Even so, Nijinsky's performance was such marvellously concentrated art that only a fool could have been shocked by it—but then, I adored the ballet myself.

Nijinsky was wholly without guile. More than that, he was naïvely—appallingly—honest. He never understood that in Society one does not always say all that one thinks. At a party in London, some time before the *Sacre du Printemps première*, Lady Ripon proposed a parlour game in which we were all to decide what sort of animal each of us most resembled—a dangerous game. Lady Ripon initiated it herself by saying that 'Diaghilev looks like a bull-dog and Stravinsky like a *renard*. Now, M. Nijinsky, what do you think I look like?' Nijinsky thought a moment, then spoke the awful, exact truth: 'Vous, Madame—chameau'— just the three words; Nijinsky did not speak much French. Lady Ripon did not expect that, of course, and in spite of her repeating: 'A camel? How amusing! I declare. Really? A camel?'—she was flustered all evening.

My own disappointment with Nijinsky was due to the fact that he did not know the musical alphabet. He never understood musical metres and he had no very certain sense of tempo. You may imagine from this the rhythmic chaos that was *Le Sacre du Printemps*, and especially the chaos of the last dance where poor Mlle Piltz, the sacrificial maiden, was not even aware of the changing bars. Nor did Nijinsky make any attempt to understand my own choreographic ideas for *Le Sacre*. In the *Danses des Adolescents*, for example, I had imagined a row of almost motionless dancers. Nijinsky made of this piece a big jumping match.

I do not say that Nijinsky's creative imagination lacked abundance; on the contrary, it was almost too rich. The point is simply that he did not know music, and therefore his notion of the relation of dance to it was primitive. To some extent this might have been remedied by education, for of course he was musical. But at the time he was made chief choreographer of the Ballet he was hopelessly incompetent in musical technique. He believed that the choreography should re-emphasize the musical beat and pattern through constant co-ordination. In effect, this restricted the dance to rhythmic duplication of the music and made of it an imitation. Choreography, as I conceive it, must realize its own form, one independent of the musical form though measured to the musical unit. Its construction will be based on whatever correspondences the choreographer may invent, but it must not seek merely to duplicate the line and beat of the music. I do not see how one can be a choreographer unless, like Balanchine, one is a musician first.

Autobiographical

If Nijinsky was the least capable musically of my choreo-graphic collaborators, his talent was elsewhere—and one talent such as he had is enough. To call him a dancer is not enough, however, for he was an even greater dramatic actor. His beautiful, but certainly not handsome, face could become the most powerful actor's mask I have ever seen and, as Petroushka, he was the most exciting human being I have ever seen on a stage.

*   *   *

I recently discovered a Nijinsky letter—addressed to me in Russia but forwarded to Switzerland, where I was then staying. It is a document of such astounding innocence—if Nijinsky hadn't written it, I think only a character in Dostoievsky might have. It seems incredible to me even now that he was so unaware of the politics and sexual jealousies and motives within the Ballet. I never saw Nijinsky again after *Le Sacre du Printemps*, so, in fact, I knew him for only four years. But those four years were the great age of the Ballet and I was with him then almost every day. I do not recall what I answered, but Diaghilev had already returned to Russia, and when I saw him on his next trip to Paris, Massine had 'replaced' poor Nijinsky.

Tuesday, 9th December 1913
1 Hidegkuti ut 51 (Budapest)

Dear Igor: I cannot hide from you what has happened to me these last months. You know that I went to South America and have not been in Europe for four months. These four months cost me dearly in money and health. My room with board cost 150 francs daily. I did not earn this money from Serge, however, but was obliged to take it from my own capital. What did Serge do all this time while we were in South America? I do not know. I wrote to him many times without receiving any answer. And I needed an answer, too, as I had worked on two new ballets—*Joseph and Potiphar*, by Strauss,[1] and another one, with Bach's music. All the preparatory work for these ballets was completed and I had only to put them in rehearsal. I could not rehearse in America because of the terrible heat, from which we almost died. How I managed to stay in good health up to the last evening there I do not know. But though I was lucky in America, here I have been ill for two months. Now I am all right.

I did not send you an invitation to my wedding as I knew you would not come, and I did not write you because I had so much to do. Please excuse me. I went with my wife to her parents' home in Budapest and there I immediately sent a telegram to Serge asking him when we could see each other. The answer to my telegram was a letter from Grigoriev[2] informing me that I shall not be asked to stage any ballets this season, and that I am not needed as an artist.

Please write to me whether this is true. I do not believe that Serge can act so meanly to me. Serge owes me a lot of money. I have received nothing for two years, neither for my dancing nor for my staging *Faune, Jeux*, and *Sacre du Printemps*. I worked for the Ballet without a contract. If it is true that Serge does not want to work with me—then I have lost everything. You understand the situation I am in. I cannot imagine what has happened, what is the reason for his behaviour. Please ask Serge what is the matter, and write to me about it. In all the newspapers of Germany, Paris, and London, etc., it is reported that I am not working any more with Diaghilev. But the whole press is against him (including the *feuilletons*). They also say that I am gathering a company of my own. In truth, I am receiving propositions from every side, and the biggest of these comes from a very rich business-

[1] Strauss's *Josephslegende*, first performed in Paris in 1914.
[2] Serge Grigoriev, the *régisseur* of the Ballet.

man, who offers one million francs to organize a new
Diaghilev[1] Russian Ballet—they wish me to have sole
artistic direction and large sums of money to commission
décors, music, etc. But I won't give them a definite answer
before I have news from you.

My numerous friends send me letters of revolt and rage
against Diaghilev—and propositions to help me and join me
in my new enterprise. I hope you will not forget me and will
answer my letter immediately.

Your loving

VASLAV

Regards to your wife and to all I know. V.

R.C. Who, then, was your most successful choreographer in the
Diaghilev period?

I.S. Bronislava Nijinska, Nijinsky's sister. Her choreography for
the original productions of *Renard* (1922) and *Noces* (1923)
pleased me more than any other works of mine interpreted by
the Diaghilev troupe. Her conception of *Noces* in blocks and
masses, and her acrobatic *Renard*, coincided with my ideas,
as well as with the real—not realistic—décors. The set of
Noces was a bees-wax yellow and the costumes were brown
peasant costumes, instead of the hideously un-Russian reds,
greens and blues one usually sees in foreign stagings of
Russian plays. *Renard* was also a real Russian satire. The
animals saluted very like the Russian Army (Orwell would have
liked this), and there was always an underlying significance to
their movements. Nijinska's *Renard* was superior in every
way to the 1929 revival, though the latter was ruined chiefly
by some jugglers Diaghilev had borrowed from a circus—an
idea of his that did not succeed at all.

Poor Bronislava had no luck with Diaghilev. Because her
face was bony and interesting, instead of doll-like, Diaghilev

[1] Sic.

was opposed to her dancing the Ballerina in *Petroushka*. And as a dancer she was second to none. Indeed, the Nijinskys—brother and sister together—were the best dancing pair imaginable. Then, later, after Nijinsky's marriage, Diaghilev could not overcome his prejudice. She looked like Nijinsky, was even shaped like him—with the same big shoulders. She was a constant reminder to him of her brother. It pained Diaghilev doubly, too, that this person who dared look like Nijinsky was a woman. You can hardly imagine how indomitable was Diaghilev's sexual prejudice. He had argued for years to convince me that the exclusive love of women was morbid (though I don't know how he could have known very much about that), that I was an incomplete artist because . . . 'morbid'. He would draw cartoons on restaurant tablecloths of steatopygous and gourd-geously mammiferous women—they looked like Dubuffet madonnas—argue about Socrates, Jesus, Leonardo da Vinci, Michelangelo (what a chaos of pederasty is Michelangelo's *Conversion of St. Paul* —including even the horse—and how unnecessary, in any case, to Paul's conversion), and go on about 'all great artists', etc. He would describe his own latest mignon in the most gratifying terms and quote Verlaine: 'Démon femelle . . .', etc. At the same time, however, he was showman enough to know how to emphasize the beauty of the female body in the ballet.

Poor Bronislava's sex, looks, and name were against her. I regretted this because, except for her and Fokine, the choreographers of my ballets were not so much dance composers as dance performers. They had been elevated to the position of choreographers not by education or experience but through being Diaghilev's *eromenoi*.[1]

---

[1] It is almost impossible to describe the perversity of Diaghilev's entourage—a kind of homosexual Swiss Guard—and the incidents and stories concerning it. I remember a rehearsal for the revival of *Renard*, in Monaco in 1929, at which our pianist—a handsome *fificus* of Diaghilev's—suddenly began looking

MASSINE

R.C. Do you remember Massine's choreography for the first *Pulcinella*?

I.S. I do and, on the whole, I considered it very good. It was sometimes mechanical, but only the variation movement was contradictory to the music. Massine had already choreographed the variations before I had scored the music, and Diaghilev had told him I would use a large orchestra with harps. Instead of this, my orchestra, as you know, is a solo woodwind quartet. In 1914—after Nijinsky's marriage—Diaghilev returned from Russia with Leonid Massine. Massine's first ballet was Strauss's *Legend of Joseph*. Of my music, besides *Pulcinella*, Massine did the choreography of the *Nightingale*. The performances of the latter were not good, however, because of insufficient orchestra rehearsals. There was a lack of co-ordination between pit and stage, and the result was unworthy of the best standards of the company.

Later, Massine did the choreography for the revival of *Le Sacre du Printemps*. I thought this excellent—incomparably clearer than Nijinsky's.

THE DIAGHILEV BALLET AND DIAGHILEV

R.C. Are there any other dancers and choreographers you would like to mention?

I.S. I should mention Idzikovsky, the great jumper and, after

very intently beyond the music rack. I followed his gaze to a Monegasque soldier in a tricorne, and then asked what the matter was. He answered: 'I long to surrender myself to him.'

Another of Diaghilev's protégés was discovered nude by the police beneath a bridge near Nice, and when one of the policemen said, 'Ou vous êtes un vicieux ou vous êtes fou,' he is supposed to have replied, 'Je suis sûrement vicieux.' And so on.

Nijinsky, the greatest Petroushka; Woizikovsky; Lopokova of the perfect technique; Karsavina, the lady of the
ballet, the first ballerina in *Petroushka* and the first Firebird
(though she should have been the Princess and Pavlova the
Firebird); Tchernicheva, a beautiful *Firebird* Princess and a
beautiful woman too—she had infatuated Alfonso XIII and
was the only woman who had attracted Ravel; Piltz, the
Russian with the German name who danced in the *Firebird*
with Fokina and Tchernicheva and was the star of the first
Sacre du Printemps; Sokolova, who danced the revival of *Le
Sacre*; Lifar, who was so beautiful as Apollo; Adolphe Bolm
who choreographed the first *Apollo* and who became my
close friend in America; George Balanchine who choreographed the first European *Apollo* (I had met him in
1925, in Nice, as he was preparing a revival of the *Chant
du Rossignol*).

*   *   *

I see that while attempting to remember the 'dancers of the
Russian Ballet' I have actually said more about Diaghilev
himself and his abnormal psychology (though I have not
exaggerated the latter) than about the Terpsichorean arts and
artists in his company. But this was inevitable since Diaghilev
was more strong-willed than all his artists and since he con-
trolled every detail of every ballet he produced.

Diaghilev was sometimes possessed by very odd and im-
practical ideas, and as he was a stubborn man, many hours of
my (and his) life were spent in trying to argue him out of
these eccentric notions. That I was not always successful,
from my point of view, is illustrated by his use of jugglers in
Renard. I did win in one important case though—*L'Histoire
du Soldat*. Diaghilev could not bear the name *L'Histoire du
Soldat* because his company had not produced it (as indeed it
could not have done in 1918, temporarily dissolved as it was

43

in the war). But in the early 1920s, he suddenly decided to stage it. His plan was eccentric. The dancers were to go about wearing advertisements, American sidewalk walking-advertisements, 'sandwich men', as they are called, or pickets. Massine would eventually have been blamed for the choreography of this undanceable ballet, but it was all Diaghilev's idea.

Diaghilev was in no sense an intellectual. He was much too sensual for that; besides, intellectuals never have any real taste—and has anyone ever had so much taste as Diaghilev? He was a deeply cultured man, however—a scholar in certain areas of art history, and an authority on Russian painting.[1] He had been a bibliophile all his life, also, and his Russian library was one of the finest in the world. But his mind was so preyed upon by superstition that he was incapable of true intellectual examination. At times I thought him pathologically superstitious. He carried amulets, he pronounced talismanic formulas; like Dr. Johnson he counted paving stones; he avoided thirteens, black cats, open ladders. Vassili, his domestic—who was always by his side holding Turkish towels, or hair brushes; but you know Cocteau's caricature —Vassili was made to perform what Diaghilev regarded as the more orthodox superstition of prayer, for while he was not a believer, he did not want to exclude the Christian possibility altogether. Vassili once told me that when they were *en route* to America in 1916, Diaghilev was so frightened by rough seas that he made him go down on his knees and pray, while he, Diaghilev, lay on his bed worrying for both—a real division of labour.

[1] Diaghilev once told me about his visit to Tolstoy to see Tolstoy's old family portraits. The old man received him cordially and showed him round his gallery with a big lantern, but his only real interest in Diaghilev was as a draughts opponent. He asked Diaghilev if he played draughts and Diaghilev said he did, so terrified was he, though he had never played in his life. They played, and of course Diaghilev did everything wrong. Tolstoy said: 'Young man, you should have told the truth right away; now go upstairs and take tea.'

Autobiographical

I remember a trip in the English Channel with him myself, and how he kept looking at a barometer, crossing himself, and saying 'Salvo, Salvo'.

*   *   *

Diaghilev feared the *iettatore* and would make the sign with the first two fingers of his right hand against its spell. Once when we were talking together in a theatre I was surprised to see his right hand occupied with the sign while he continued to talk to me, so to speak with his left hand. 'Seriosha, what are you doing?' I asked. He pointed to three men behind him and said that one of them had the *malocchio*. I looked and saw that he was mistaken and told him so, but he would not abandon the digital counter-influence until the three men had gone.

Diaghilev was self-destructively vain. He starved himself for the sake of his figure. I remember him—the next to last time I saw him—opening his overcoat and proudly showing me how slender he had become. This was for the benefit of one of his last protégés—a modest, self-effacing, and utterly ruthless careerist who was about as fond of Diaghilev as Herod was of children. Diaghilev was a diabetic, but he was not saved by insulin (he feared injections and preferred to take his chances with the disease). I do not know the medical explanation of his death, but I do know that this event was a terrible shock to me, the more so because I had broken with him over *Le Baiser de la Fée* (which, as I have said, Ida Rubinstein had staged, and which he had very bitterly criticized), and because we were not reconciled when he died.

I have recently uncovered a packet of letters and other documents addressed to me at the time of Diaghilev's death. One of the documents is a German newspaper describing Diaghilev as *ein berühmter Tanzer*. I quote two of the letters.

Autobiographical

Antequeruela Alta 11,

Granada,

22nd August 1929

Bien cher Igor, I am profoundly moved by the death of Diaghilev and it is my wish to write to you before I speak to anyone else. What a terrible loss for you. Of all the admirable things he did, the first was his revelation of you. We owe him that above all. And without you, besides, the Ballet couldn't have existed. . . . However, it is a consolation that our poor friend died without surviving his work. I always remember his fears during the war that someone might come and take his place. Later we understood how useless were such fears, for of course no one could ever take his place. And now I beg one favour of you: please give my most passionate condolences to the head of the Diaghilev Ballet, whoever that is now. I ask you to do this because I do not know anyone there now who could receive them.

I embrace you with all my old and true affection,

Manuel de Falla

P.S. I hope you received my last letter which I sent registered, thinking you might be absent.

The second letter is from Walter Nouvel, the secretary of the Ballet and Diaghilev's most intimate friend since they were students together in St. Petersburg University. Nouvel's sensibilities were similar to Diaghilev's (indeed, he used to say: 'I like Italians; they recognize one right away; everyone in Italy always says "grazie, tante" to me'). His calm and intelligence saved the Ballet more than once. He was a good musician too, and to me personally the kindest of friends.

Autobiographical

My dear Igor, I was touched to my soul by your deeply-felt letter. We are sharing the same sorrow. I am bereft of a man to whom I was tied by a friendship of forty years. But I am happy today that I never failed to be faithful to this friendship. Many things united us and many things separated us. Often I suffered from him, often I was revolted by him, but now that he is in the grave all is forgotten and all is forgiven. And, I understand now that no ordinary measure of the conduct of human relations could be applied to so exceptional a man. He lived and died 'one of the favoured of God'. But he was a heathen, and a Dionysian heathen, not an Apollonian. He loved all earthly things: earthly love, earthly passions, earthly beauty. The sky was for him no more than a beautiful cupola above a beautiful earth.

This does not mean that he was without mysticism. No, but his mysticism was that of a pagan, not of a Christian, order. With him, Faith was replaced by a deep superstition; he had no fear of God but was terrified before the elements and their mysteries; he possessed no Christian humility but was instead a man of sensual, almost childlike emotions and feelings. His death, a pagan's death, was beautiful. He died in love and beauty and under the smiles of those two gods he swore by, and served his whole life, with such passion. Such a man must be loved by Christ.

I embrace you,

WALTER NOUVEL

Autobiographical

These are four letters from Diaghilev to me:

1

Firenze,
Quattro viale Torricelli,
1st November 1914

You awful pig. I wire you that I have signed the American contract, and that Mestrovic[1] answered that he expected me in Rome in November. And you, not a word. You force me, an old man, to take to my pen. We stay here until 10th November, then go to Rome. We were in Ravenna and were overwhelmed by this magnificent cemetery. I have received a mad telegram from Misia saying she will not leave Paris because it is now the most beautiful city in the world. I have received a telegram from Nijinsky, too. He has no right to leave Budapest for the moment because of the war. Prokofiev is working with Gorodetsky and it seems he will finish his piano concerto. Kussevitsky is going to conduct in Rome and I shall see him. I received from your Mr. Fokine an amiable inquiry about my affairs. The Fokines are at Biarritz. Well, and you, which tableau of *Noces* have you reached? Write, Dog.

Yours,   SERIOSHA

2

Grand Hotel, Roma,
25th November 1914

Dear Igor,

Our concert did not work out for some last-minute reason. When I originally proposed it to San Martino[2] he jumped up

[1] The ballet Diaghilev had planned with Mestrovic was *Liturgie*. I went to Rome for two weeks as his guest to discuss the project with him and with Mestrovic, but I refused to do the ballet, both because I disapproved of the idea of presenting the Mass as a ballet spectacle, and because Diaghilev wanted me to compose it and *Les Noces* for the same price.

[2] President of the Santa Cecilia.

9. Nijinsky, Isola Bella, June, 1912

10. Myself, *ibidem*, looking like a Bersagliere. I was on holiday, just having finished *Le Sacre du Printemps*. These two photographs (numbers 9 and 10) are by Diaghilev

11. With Ravel, Clarens, 1913

on his divan in transports and shouted 'but I will take
Stravinsky with four hands'. Then when I saw him next time
he told me how good it was to be an absolute Tsar and
boasted that he could invite you without asking anybody. All
details were settled and the concert arranged for the third of
January when suddenly I received a letter with the following:
'. . . as to the fee, you can imagine in what an embarrassing
condition the Academy finds itself in a season like this, when
it has so few resources. On the other hand, Stravinsky is
young and since he is not trying to make a regular conductor's career I hope he will be satisfied with a very modest sum
which could be between six and seven hundred francs.' I
hastened to San Martino and explained to him that the train
ticket costs 240 francs and your sojourn in Rome seven days
at 50 francs a day, 350, *id est* 600 francs, the sum he proposed.
All that I can do is to invite you to stay with me so you will
have no expenses in Rome, and argue you into accepting
1,200 francs. He agreed with me and said that to get the
money he will shrink his budget (!!) (he has also invited
Strauss, Debussy, and Kussevitsky from Moscow and
others) so that the concert could take place. I even spoke with
him and with their conductor about the order of the programme and I insisted that they give you twelve rehearsals.
Then I received this note from him:

'My dear friend, as to Stravinsky's concert I regret very
much to have to cancel it for reasons which I will explain to
you with my own voice on my return.'

He went for three days to Turin and I shall see him at
Sunday's concert. I will propose to him the following: to take
on your travelling expenses myself and ask him to pay you
1,000 francs. If this also fails to work out, then to hell with
him.

We absolutely must see each other. You must come here
for two weeks—the best time would be from about the

twentieth of December. If you pass the holidays here, you can have a little, quiet room in our apartment, and one eats not badly here. But you must come: our plan with Mestrovic is progressing. Mestrovic is a timid man with an exaggerated *amour-propre* and a distrust of everything one does. He has genius in fulfilling his work, but his advice is mediocre. His intentions are always good, and he is inflamed by ideas. But we must take care ourselves about everything. Your being at such a distance makes this all impossibly difficult. I work together with him and Massine; bless us, I want Massine to stage this ballet!

Nijinsky behaves so stupidly.[1] He didn't even answer my detailed and, in my opinion, fair letter, and to my modest telegram requesting, 'reply paid', whether he had received it, he answered only: 'Letter received. Cannot come.'

I am sure that his wife is busy making him into the first ballet master of the Budapest Opera. As for *Noces*, do not worry. I will write him a second, less modest and less reasonable letter and this miserable person will understand that now is not the moment for joking. The invention of movement in *Noces* is definitely for Nijinsky, but I will not discuss the thing with him for several months yet. As for Massine, he is still too young, but each day he becomes more and more ours, and this is important. I am not going into any details now but let me tell you that what I have in mind is a performance of the MASS in six or seven short tableaux. The epoch will be Byzantine, which Mestrovic will arrange in his own way. The music should be a series of *a cappella* sacred choruses, inspired, perhaps, by Gregorian chant, but more of that later. When you come you will meet a great connoisseur of these matters—Mestrovic.

---

[1] Diaghilev's vengeance had begun. Almost every letter from him for the next few years contained a complaint about Nijinsky, and when Nijinsky wrote to him from N.Y. addressing him 'tu', he was more offended than ever.

Autobiographical

The frescos in the Roman underground churches of the first century are really astounding.

For the moment, that is all. I hope you approve. The main thing is that you come. Please answer me immediately at the Grand Hotel.

I embrace you,

SERGE

3

Grand Hotel
(*we are in the Grand Hotel until 8th March*)
3rd March 1915

Dear, you are a little mad. San Martino buy something? His wife would choke to death first. They'll never do it. However, the American Russell was here; he found the price very high, though he said he would try to do something if you would send him a manuscript. He has gone to America, and his address is c/o Metropolitan Opera House, New York, Henry Russell, Esquire.

I am afraid to send him the manuscript, however, because someone could print it in America without paying you a penny. If you want to, however, do it yourself. I on my side will speak to Ricordi, although with little hope. As to the material of the *Nightingale*, you are not so much mad as ridiculous. If Teliatina[1] stages it at all he will not do so earlier than 1917, when everybody will have forgotten about the war. Why in hell should Prokofiev (who is coming today) drag the material with him so that it can stay two years in Petrogrrrrrad?[2] Tell me if we have to fulfil this foolish order.

Now about us. We are going to Naples and Palermo on 8th March for 10-12 days and afterwards coming to you to

---

[1] Teliakovsky, Director of the Opera in St. Petersburg. Teliatina means veal.
[2] Diaghilev is making fun of the word as we all did when the 'St.' was dropped and the 'burg' made 'grad'.

51

take *Les Noces*. It must be finished by that time. Then, with you, or without you, we are going for about three weeks to Spain. And afterwards? I don't know what and where, but we shall work, and not twiddle our thumbs as some people do. So, expect us about the twentieth of March, and have a big ballet ready—without that I shall be very angry.

Before speaking with Dalcroze we must see what his material is.[1]

Everybody greets you. You left an 'indelible mark', as they say here.

SERGE D.

P.S. Khvotschinsky leaves for the war, drafted in Russia.

P.P.S. It is as hot as summer here, and the sun beats down full force.

4

Hotel de Paris,
Monto Carlo,
7th April 1926

Mon cher Igor, I read your letter in tears. Not for a single minute have I ever stopped thinking of you except as a brother. Therefore, I feel joyful and full of light today because in your thoughts you have embraced me as one. I remember the letter you wrote me after the death of your brother Goury. I remember also the letter I wrote you not long ago telling you that when in moments of deep disturbance I remember that you are living almost next door in the world, I start to feel better. To forgive, it seems to me, is within the power of God alone; only He can judge. But we other little lecherous people, we ought in our moments of quarrelling or repentance to have enough strength to embrace each other

---

[1] I don't remember what Dalcroze's project was, but I do remember having been to him and having seen demonstrations of his eurhythmic gymnastics.

like brothers and forget. This can evoke the thirst for for-
giveness, and if you have this thirst, turn it towards me. I do
not fast or go to confession or Communion (I am not a
communicant). However, I ask you to forgive me my sins,
voluntary and involuntary, and to keep in your heart only
this feeling of brotherly love which I feel towards you.

SERIOSHA

3

SOME RUSSIAN COMPOSERS

RIMSKY-KORSAKOV

R.C. What are your present feelings, personal and otherwise, towards Rimsky-Korsakov, and do you remember the *Chant
Funèbre* you composed in his memory?

I.S. After fifty years it is quite impossible to discriminate between
memories personal and impersonal; all memories are personal, yet mine are removed so far from the person that they
cannot be told otherwise than impersonally. Few people can
have been as close to Rimsky as I was, especially after the
death of my father, when, for me, he was like an adopted
parent. We try not to judge our parents, but we judge them,
none the less, and often unjustly. I hope I am not unjust to
Rimsky.

$$*\qquad\qquad *\qquad\qquad *$$

A great difference in character existed between the Rimsky
of the Autobiography, which is the one most people knew,
and the Rimsky who was my teacher. Readers of that well-
written but matter-of-fact book think of him as someone not
very easy with his sympathy and not abundantly generous or
kind; moreover, the artist in the Autobiography was sometimes shockingly shallow in his artistic aims. My Rimsky was
deeply sympathetic, however, deeply and unshowingly
generous, and unkind only to admirers of Tchaikovsky. The

54

shallow I cannot counter, for obviously there was nothing profound either in Rimsky's nature or in his music.

I adored Rimsky but did not like his 'mentality', by which I mean his almost bourgeois atheism (he would call it his 'rationalism'). His mind was closed to any religious or metaphysical idea. If conversation happened to touch on some point of religion or philosophy he would simply refuse to allow that point to be considered in the light of 'revealed religion'. I was accustomed to dine with the Rimsky-Korsakov family after my lessons. We drank vodka and ate *zakousky* together, then started the dinner. I would sit next to Rimsky and often continue to discuss some problem from my previous lesson. Rimsky's sons and daughters occupied the rest of the table. His second son, Andrei, had studied philosophy at Heidelberg, and he often came to dinner with one Mironov, a university friend. But in spite of these young people's interest in philosophy, Rimsky would permit no discussion of it in his presence. I remember someone introducing 'Resurrection' as a table topic, and Rimsky drawing a zero on the tablecloth as he said, 'there is nothing after death, death is the end'. I then had the temerity to suggest that perhaps this was also merely one point of view, but was made to feel for some time thereafter that I should have held my peace.

I thought I had found friends in Rimsky's younger sons, two young gentlemen who, at least in provincial St. Petersburg, were beacons of enlightenment. Andrei, a man three years my senior and a 'cellist of some ability, was especially kind to me, though this kindness lasted only while his father was alive; after the success of the *Firebird* in 1910 he, and in fact the entire Rimsky-Korsakov family, turned against me.[1] He even reviewed *Petroushka* for a Russian newspaper dismissing it as 'Russian vodka with French perfumes'. Vladimir, his brother,

[1] I think this was musical rather than personal. My music was too 'advanced' for them. Glazunov was their darling.

was a competent violinist and I owe to him my first knowledge of violin fingerings. I was not close to Sophie and Nadejda, Rimsky's daughters,[1] though my last contact with the Rimsky-Korsakov family was through Nadezhda's husband, Maximilian Steinberg, who had come to Paris in 1924 and heard me play my piano concerto there. But you may imagine his response to that work when I tell you that the best he could do even for my *Fireworks* was to shrug his shoulders. After hearing the concerto he wanted to lecture me about the whole of my mistaken career. He returned to Russia thoroughly annoyed when I refused to see him.

*   *   *

Rimsky was a tall man, like Berg, or Aldous Huxley, and like Huxley, too, he suffered from poor eyesight. He wore blue-tinted spectacles, sometimes keeping an extra pair on his forehead, a habit of his I have caught. When conducting an orchestra he would bend over the score, and, hardly ever looking up, wave the baton in the direction of his knees. His difficulty in seeing the score was so great, and he was so absorbed in listening, that he gave almost no directions to the orchestra at all. Like Berg, he suffered from asthma. In the last year of his life he began to fail very suddenly from the effects of this disease, and though he was only sixty-four years old we were aware that he would not last very long. He had a series of severe attacks in January 1908. Telephone calls came every morning from his house to ours, and I waited every morning not knowing whether he was still alive.

Rimsky was a strict man and a strict, though at the same time very patient, teacher (he would say '*ponimyete, poni-myete*', 'you understand', again and again throughout my lessons). His knowledge was precise, and he was able to im-

[1] My *Pastorale* was written with Nadezhda's voice in mind, and dedicated to her. I later arranged this piece for violin and four woodwinds for the simple reason that songs as such were no longer performed.

part whatever he knew with great clarity. His teaching was all 'technical'. But, whereas he knew valuable details about harmony and practical orchestral writing, what he knew about composition itself was not all it should have been. He was for me, when I first came to him, *sans reproche* musically, but before very long I began to wish for someone even less 'reproachable' and for music that would satisfy the ideals of my growing mind as Rimsky's was failing to do. The revival of polyphony and the renewal of form that had begun in Vienna in the very year of Rimsky's death were developments entirely unknown to the Rimsky school. I am grateful to Rimsky for many things, and I do not wish to blame him for what he did not know; nevertheless, the most important tools of my art I had to discover for myself. I should mention, too, that by the time I had become his pupil he was a reactionary who would oppose on principle anything new that came from France or Germany. I never ceased to be surprised by this attitude since outside the arts he was a radical, anti-Tsarist progressive.

*   *   *

Though Rimsky had wit and a lively sense of humour, though he had developed a literary style of his own, his literary taste was parochial, and in the worst sense. The librettos of his operas, except that of *The Snow Maiden* (Ostrovsky) and *Mozart and Salieri* (Pushkin), are, on the whole, embarrassingly bad. I once drew his attention to an anachronism in one of them: 'But, dear master, do you really think such an expression was in use in the fifteenth century?' 'It is in use now and that is all we need concern ourselves with.' Rimsky could not conceive of Tchaikovsky otherwise than as a 'rival'. Tchaikovsky had been more influential in Germany than Rimsky, and Rimsky was jealous (it seems to me that Tchaikovsky had a distinct influence on Mahler; listen to Figs. 16 to 21 in the fourth movement of Mahler's first symphony, and from Fig. 21 in the fifth movement of the second symphony). He would say, and never tire of saying, 'Tchaikovsky's music is in abominable taste', and indeed, though much of it is, Rimsky might have realized that his own music could share honours with Tchaikovsky's on this count. Nevertheless, Rimsky was proud to exhibit in his work-room a large silver crown Tchaikovsky had given him for the *première* of the *Capriccio Espagnol*. Tchaikovsky had attended the dress rehearsal and had so admired the brilliance of the music that he presented Rimsky with this token of homage the next day.

Rimsky was an Anglophile. He had learned English during his term as a naval officer, and though I cannot say how well he spoke it, I first heard the language from his lips. He often expressed himself in little English asides. Thus, one day a young composer had come to show him a score, but in his nervous excitement lost it in a droshky. Rimsky groaned dis-appointment in Russian, but whispered to me in English, 'The heavens are merciful.'

Rimsky did not mention me in his Autobiography for the reason that he did not wish to show me any mark of deference; he had many pupils and was always careful to avoid favouri-tism. My brother Goury *is* mentioned because he had sung in a cantata which I composed for Rimsky and which was per-formed in his house. After this event Rimsky wrote my mother a charming letter in appreciation of our talents.

Rimsky attended my first two *premières* with me. The first of these pieces, the Symphony in E Flat, is dedicated to him (the manuscript is still with his family). It was performed in St. Petersburg on 27th April 1907; I remember the date because my Uncle Ielatchitch presented me with a medal commemorat-ing it. Rimsky sat next to me and, from time to time, made critical remarks: 'this is too heavy; be more careful when you use trombones in their middle register'. As the concert took place at noon, and as the audience was not a paying one, I cannot say whether the applause I heard signified a success. The only bad omen was Glazunov, who came to me afterwards saying, 'very nice, very nice'. The Imperial Kapellmeister Varlich, a general in uniform, conducted the performance. My second *première*, *Le Faune et la Bergère*, conducted by Felix Blumenfeld later the same year in one of Belayev's Russian Symphony Concerts, must have irritated Rimsky's conservatism, however, incredible though that may now seem. He found the first song 'strange', and my use of wholetone progressions suspiciously 'Debussy-ist'. 'There, you see,' he said to me after the performance, 'I have heard it, but if I were to hear it again in a half-hour I would have to make the same effort of adjustment all over again.' At this time, Rimsky's own 'modernism' was based on a few flimsy enharmonic devices.

The *Chant Funèbre* for wind instruments that I composed in Rimsky's memory was performed in a concert conducted by Blumenfeld in St. Petersburg shortly after Rimsky's death. I remember the piece as the best of my works before the *Firebird*, and the most advanced in chromatic harmony. The orchestral parts must have been preserved in one of the St. Petersburg orchestral libraries; I wish someone in Leningrad would look for the parts, for I would be curious myself to see what I was composing just before the *Firebird*. Alas, the only homage I have paid Rimsky since then was my conducting of his tone poem *Sadko*[1] (not the opera; the tone poem is a more interesting work than the opera), the one work of his which I thought worth resurrecting.

*   *   *

I no longer possess any of Rimsky's letters to me, though I

[1] In New York, in 1935.

must have had fifty or more in Oustiloug. I regret this very much as he had sent me many delightful cards from Lago di Garda, where he spent his summers. I have no manuscript either, though he gave me the first fifty pages of his *Snow Maiden* score. In fact, I have no autograph of his at all— which information is for the benefit of the person who regularly sends me registered letters from somewhere in Brazil begging for an autograph of Rimsky's.

CÉSAR CUI

R.C. Did you know César Cui in your Rimsky-Korsakov years?

I.S. I must have known him very early in my life for he was a great admirer of my father's and probably a guest at our home. My father had sung in some of Cui's operas and I remember being sent to Cui in 1901 with a special invitation to an opera performance celebrating my father's Jubilee—my father's wish to pay Cui a mark of attention. But though I saw Cui frequently at concerts I do not remember him dressed otherwise than in a military uniform—trousers with a stripe on the side, and a tunic which on special occasions had a little balcony of medals. Cui continued to lecture at the Military Institute in St. Petersburg until the end of his life. He was said to be an authority on fortifications. Indeed, I suspect he knew more about them than about counterpoint, and the impression in my mind of Cui as a kind of Clausewitz is as strong as the impression of the musician. He was stiff and military personally, too, and one felt half-inclined to stand at attention when talking to him. He could be seen at concerts and other musical functions in St. Petersburg almost regularly, in spite of his age, and the musicians of my generation came to stare at him as at a great curiosity.

Cui was rabidly anti-Wagner, but he had little to advance

in Wagner's stead—a case of 'more substance in our enmities than in our love'. Nor could I take his orientalism seriously. 'Russian music', or 'Hungarian' or 'Spanish', or any other of the national nineteenth-century kind is, all of it, as thin as local colour and as boring. Cui did help me to discover Dargomizhsky, however, and for that I am grateful. *Russalka* was the popular Dargomizhsky opera at the time, but Cui considered *The Stone Guest* the better work. His writings drew my attention to the remarkable quality of the recitatives in the latter, and though I do not know what I would think of this music now, it has had an influence on my subsequent operatic thinking.

I do not know whether Cui had heard my *Firebird*, and though I think he was present at the first performances of the *Scherzo Fantastique* and *Fireworks*, I recall no hint of his reactions to these pieces reaching my ears.

ANTON ARENSKY

.C. And Anton Arensky?

S. Arensky was a composer of the Moscow school—in other words, a follower of Tchaikovsky. I—as a pupil of Rimsky-Korsakov, and for that very reason—could not know him well. And, in all that concerned Arensky, Rimsky was, I thought, unjustifiably harsh and unkind. He criticized Arensky's music captiously and unnecessarily, and a comment about it, which he allowed to be printed after Arensky's death, was cruel: 'Arensky did very little, and that little will soon be forgotten.' I attended a performance of Arensky's opera *Dream on the Volga* with Rimsky. The music was dull indeed, and Arensky's attempt to evoke sinister atmosphere with the bass clarinet was horse-opera farce. But Rimsky's exclamation to me that 'the noble bass clarinet should not be put to such ignominious use' must have been overheard several rows in front of us, and later, of course, throughout the theatre.

Arensky had been friendly, interested, and helpful to me, however, and in spite of Rimsky I always liked him and at least one of his works—the famous piano trio. He meant something to me also by the mere fact of his being a direct personal link with Tchaikovsky.

SERGE TANEYEV

R.C. And Serge Taneyev?

I.S. I saw Taneyev from time to time—as often, that is, as he came to St. Petersburg, for he too was a Muscovite. He was a Tchaikovsky disciple also, and he sometimes took Tchaikovsky's classes for him at the Moscow Conservatory. Taneyev was a good teacher, and his treatise on counterpoint —one of the best books of its kind—was highly valued by me in my youth. I could respect Taneyev as a composer, especially for certain passages in his opera *The Oresteia*, and I admired him greatly as a pianist. But the same hostility prevailed on the Rimsky-Korsakov side and poor Taneyev was very unjustly treated in St. Petersburg. I might add that Taneyev was held in some awe by us for an extra-musical reason: he was widely acknowledged to be the best friend of the Countess Tolstoy.

ANATOL LIADOV

R.C. What were your relations with Anatol Liadov—especially after you had accepted the *Firebird* commission he had failed to fulfil?

I.S. Liadov was a darling man, as sweet and charming as his own

Autobiographical

Musical Snuff Box. We called him 'the blacksmith', but I can't think why unless it was because he was so soft and gentle and so very unlike a blacksmith. He was a small man with a sympathetic, squinting face and few hairs on his head. He always carried books under his arm—Maeterlinck, E.T.A. Hoffmann, Andersen: he liked tender, fantastical things. He was a short-winded, pianissimo composer and he never could have written a long and noisy ballet like the *Firebird*. He was more relieved than offended I suspect when I accepted the commission.

I liked Liadov's music, especially the piano pieces, *Kikimora* and the *Baba-Yaga.* He had a good harmonic sense and he always presented his music well instrumentally. Perhaps I was even somehow aware of the *Musical Snuff Box* when I composed a similar piece of my own, the 'ice-cream' wagon *Valse* in my second suite for small orchestra. I often accompanied Liadov to concerts, but if we were not together and he happened to see me in the hall he would always invite me to come and follow a score with him. I do not know if he had heard the *Firebird* in later years, but I am sure he would have defended it if he had. He was the most progressive of the musicians of his generation and he had championed my first pieces. Early in Scriabin's career, when the larger public's resistance to that composer was still general, someone referred to Scriabin in Liadov's (and my) presence as a fool, whereupon Liadov said: 'I like such fools.'

*   *   *

When I think of Liadov I remember another composer, and since it will not occur to you to question me about him, I will mention him myself. Joseph Wihtol, composer and teacher—he had collaborated with Rimsky-Korsakov in one or two works and was a colleague of Liadov's in that horrible musical prison, the St. Petersburg Conservatory—was kindly like

63

Liadov and very helpful to me. He was a jovial man, with round face and round hands like a cat's paws. He later lived in Riga, and when I visited that city on a concert tour in 1934 his affection and hospitality to me were princely.

SCRIABIN

R.C. What were your associations with Scriabin, both in St. Petersburg, and later, when Diaghilev had become interested in him? Did he have any influence on you?

I.S. I do not remember my first meeting with Scriabin, but it must have been in Rimsky-Korsakov's house, for we often encountered each other there in the years of my tutelage with Rimsky. But he was personally so maladroit and his way of treating me and Rimsky's other pupils *von oben bis unten* was so detestable that I never wished to cultivate his company. Rimsky disliked him too; in fact, whenever he mentioned Scriabin to me he referred to him as 'the narcissus'. Rimsky did not value Scriabin's gifts as a composer very highly either: '*mais, c'est du Rubinstein*' ('Anton Rubinstein' being at this time a term of abuse equivalent to *merde*).

As a pupil of Taneyev, Scriabin was better grounded in counterpoint and harmony than most of the Russians—very much better equipped in these respects than, say, Prokofiev whose gifts were perhaps more brilliant. His own ground was derived in part from Liszt, which was natural for the age. I had nothing against Liszt, but I did not like Scriabin's way of continually arguing a Chopin-Liszt line as against a German tradition. I have elsewhere described his shock when I expressed my admiration for Schubert. The marvellous Schubert F minor Fantasia for piano four-hands was for Scriabin *la musique pour les jeunes demoiselles*. But most of his musical opinions were no better than that. I last saw him in Ouchy

12. Ravel, Nijinsky, Bronislava Nijinska, photographed by me on Ravel's balcony, 1913

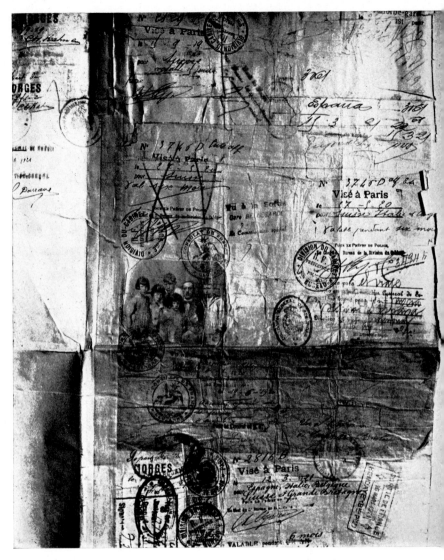

13. A page of my Tsarist passport

shortly before his death: his father was Russian Consul in Lausanne and I had gone to Lausanne to have my passport signed. Alexander Nicolaevitch had just arrived there. He talked to me about Debussy and Ravel, and about my own music. He had no insight at all: 'I can show you how to make their kind of French grimace. Take a figure of open fifths, relieve it with augmented $\frac{6}{3}$ chords, add a tower of thirds until you have dissonance enough, then repeat the whole thing in another "key": you will be able to compose as much "Debussy" and "Ravel" as you wish.' He did not tell me all that he told others about my own music, namely, that he, too, was horrified by *Le Sacre*; but as he had not been able to follow either *Petroushka* or the *Firebird* it was my fault to have been surprised.

Scriabin's vogue in St. Petersburg began about 1905. I attributed it more to his phenomenal abilities as a pianist than to whatever new qualities there were in his music, but no matter the reasons, there *was* a sudden and very considerable interest in him, and he was hailed, at least in *avant-garde* circles, as an 'original'.

*   *   *

To answer your question, perhaps I have been influenced by Scriabin in one very insignificant respect, in the piano writing of my Etudes, op. 7. But one is influenced by what one loves, and I never could love a bar of his bombastic music. As for Scriabin's short career with Diaghilev, I know only why it was short: Scriabin was 'morbid'. Diaghilev had mistakenly assumed the contrary, and had decided to take him to Paris, telling me, 'I will show Scriabin's music to Paris.' The show, whatever it was, did not succeed.

Scriabin was literary-minded. Villiers de l'Isle Adam, Huysmans, the whole company of the 'decadents' were his rages. It was the age of Symbolism, and in Russia he and

E

Konstantin Balmont were its gods. He was a follower of Mme Blavatsky, too, and a serious and well-considered theosophist himself. I did not understand this, for in my generation Mme Blavatksy was already very *démodée*, but I respected his beliefs. Scriabin was an arrogant-looking man with thick blond hair and a blond *barbiche*. Although his death was tragic and premature, I have sometimes wondered at the kind of music such a man would have written had he survived into the 1920s.

SERGE PROKOFIEV

R.C. What are your personal memories of Prokofiev, and what did you think of each other's music?

I.S. I met Prokofiev in St. Petersburg in the winter of 1906-7. He was only seventeen or eighteen at the time, but he had been given part of a concert in Walter Nouvel's 'Evenings of Contemporary Music' series in which to play a group of his piano pieces. His performance was remarkable—but I have always liked his music hearing him play it—and the music had personality. I do not know if Rimsky was there, though I do remember from a conversation with him about Prokofiev that he regarded him very sceptically. But it was Liadov, not Rimsky-Korsakov, who had been Prokofiev's protector.

I did not know Prokofiev well until several years later, in Milan, during the war. Diaghilev was busy introducing him to the Futurists and to 'leftist' circles in general. Diaghilev wanted him to mix, to exchange ideas with other artists, but the attempt failed as it always did thereafter because Prokofiev was full of splinters, as he says about his music in a letter to me, with people who were more cultivated than he was—and a good many were that. On this Milanese visit *Le Sacre du Printemps* was his only subject of conversation. He adored *Le Sacre* and was for many years quite unable to recover from the effect of it.

Prokofiev was the contrary of a musical thinker. He was, in fact, startlingly naïve in matters of musical construction. He had some technique and he could do certain things very well, but more than that, he had personality; one saw that in his every gesture—biological personality let us call it. His musical judgments were usually commonplace, however, and often wrong. An example of the latter comes to mind in relation to *Petroushka*. He was once seated beside me at a performance of that work when, in the fourth tableau, at the climax of the Russian dances, he turned to me and said, 'You should have ended here.' But it is obvious to any perceptive musician that the best pages in *Petroushka* are the last.

Prokofiev was always very Russian-minded and always primitively anti-clerical. But in my opinion these dispositions had little to do with his return to Russia. The latter was a sacrifice to the bitch goddess, and nothing else. He had had no success in the United States or Europe for several seasons, while his visit to Russia had been a triumph. When I saw him for the last time, in New York in 1937, he was despondent about his material and artistic fate in France. He was politically naïve, however, and had learned nothing from the example of his good friend Miakovsky. He returned to Russia, and when finally he understood his situation there, it was too late. A few weeks before his death a friend of mine in Paris received a letter from him inquiring about me, and this touched me very much.

*   *   *

I do not know what he liked of my music beyond the Russian pieces, and especially *Le Sacre*, *Renard*, *Noces*, but I doubt if he knew very much of what I had written in the 1930s, and I am quite sure he would not have liked it if he did. The fact that we were not really in accord musically did not seem to matter. We were always on very good terms, there was never any incident between us, and I believe he liked me as much as he did any musical friend. But one could see Prokofiev a thousand times without establishing any profound connection with him, and we rarely discussed music when we were together. I used to think that Prokofiev's depths were engaged only when he played chess. He was a master player and he played with all the celebrities, as well as with my wife, Vera.

Diaghilev had believed at first that Prokofiev would develop into a great composer, and he held to this belief for several years. Then, finally, he confided to me that he was beginning to think him 'stupid'. I have a letter from Diaghilev about Prokofiev:

Grand Hotel, Rome,
8th March 1915

Dear Igor, Many new questions, but first of all Prokofiev. Yesterday he played in the Augusteum, and with some success, but that is not the point. The point is, he brought me about one-third of the music of his new ballet. The subject is a St. Petersburg fabrication; it would have been good for the Mariinsky Theatre ten years ago, but is not for us. The music, as he says, does not look for Russianism, it is just music. Precisely, just music, and very bad. Now we have to start all over again, and for this we have to be kindly with him and keep him with us for two or three months. I am counting on your help. He is talented, but what do you expect when the most cultivated person he sees is Tcherepnine who impresses him with his *avant-gardisme* (!) He is easily influenced and it seems to me he is a much nicer person than we suspected he would be after his arrogant appearance in the past. I will bring him to you. He must be changed entirely, otherwise we will lose him forever. . . .

Autobiographical

Of Prokofiev's Diaghilev ballets I preferred *Chout*, though the *L'Enfant prodigue* by Balanchine was the most beautiful choreographically. But I do not wish to criticize Prokofiev: I should be silent if I could say nothing good about such a man. Prokofiev *had* merits, and that rare thing, the instant imprint of personality. Nor was he cheap—facility is not the same thing as cheapness. Only, alas, he would not have understood Mallarmé's reply to a man who had congratulated him upon making such a clear speech: 'Then I will have to add some shadows.'

*   *   *

Prokofiev's letters to me were very affectionate. It is hard to reproduce their tone in English, but I think this example gives some idea of the character of his correspondence:

> *c/o Haensel and Jones,*
> *33 West 42nd St., New York,*
> *10th December 1919*

Dear Stravinsky,

I tell you the following with pleasure. Yesterday your *Pribaoutki* were performed for the first time in America. Vera Janacopulos sang, a very talented singer.[1] Her approach to them was most loving and she sang them beautifully except perhaps for *Uncle Armand* which is too low for her voice. The success was very great and all four songs were repeated. Lots of people in the audience laughed, but gaily, not indignantly. I sat next to Fokine and we bawled 'bravos' as loud as we could. The instrumentalists played well, and performed their tasks with interest. Only the viola and the bass may have been angry about it. The flautist, who has already played the *Japanese Lyrics,* was so sure of himself, no difficulties could frighten him. I went to the rehearsals and tried to explain what was not clear to them. Personally I like most: 1. *Uncle*

---

[1] I knew her well.

Armand. The oboe and clarinet are like the gurgle of a bottle emptying. You express drunkenness through your clarinet with the skill of a real drunkard; 2. The whole *Natashka*, but especially the last five bars with the delightful grumbling of the winds; 3. *The Colonel*, entirely, but especially the oboe twitters and the climax on the words 'paea propala', etc.; 4. Many things in the last song, but the coda above all: the clarinet's G-A natural and the English horn's A flat are most excellent and most insolent.

I send you my cordial greetings and best wishes. I shall be very happy to hear from you,

Yours,

S. PROKOFIEV

PORTRAITS MÉMOIRES

PORTRAITS MÉMOIRES

PAUL VALÉRY

R.C. Your long friendship and admiration for Paul Valéry are well known. Would you tell me what you remember of him and also what you now think of his work?

S. I met Paul Valéry for the first time in 1921 or 1922: while only half recalling the date and the occasion (a reception by the Princess Edmond de Polignac, I think) I do remember the meeting. Valéry was small, about my own height in fact, which for some reason surprised me. He was quick, quiet (he spoke in rapid, *sotto voce* mumbles), and extremely gentle. He seemed a terrible dandy at first sight because of his monocle and *boutonnière*, but that impression dissolved as soon as he began to talk. Wit and intelligence were in everything he said, though not merely in what he said: they were manifest in his whole person. This was to be expected of Valéry, of course; what I did not expect, however, but was delighted to discover in him that first day, was a truly joyful sense of humour. By the time of parting we had already attained a high state of personal sympathy, and we were ever after natural friends.

73

Now that I have begun to force my memory about Valéry, I wonder I did not know him earlier. I had read *Monsieur Teste* before the 1914 war. I remember that I mentioned the book to Gide and that Gide responded with an encomium about its author. Ravel had also talked to me about Valéry in those years, and C. F. Ramuz too, though somewhat later, in Switzerland during the war. And we had many mutual friends (Misia Sert, for example) at whose homes we ought to have encountered each other. But whatever kept us apart, we never failed to make up the gaps, and in the later 1920s and in the 30s up to my departure for America, we saw each other so regularly that we might be thought to have formed a 'circle'. When I left Europe in September 1939 to give the Norton Lectures at Harvard, I counted Valéry of all my friends the one whose wisdom I would most sorely miss.

Valéry was a deep source of intellectual and moral support to me on two important occasions in my life. One of these concerned the Harvard lectures, *The Poetics of Music*, as I call them. I had asked him to read and criticize my manuscript. I was anxious to have his comments on its literary style, especially since I had written the lectures not in my own language but in French; I was not quite confident about some of the 'writing'. Accordingly, I read my manuscript to him in a country house near Paris, sometime in the late summer of 1939. He suggested various changes in the phrasing and order of words, but to my great relief endorsed the style of the lectures without reservation.

My other 'professional' call on him came at the time of the first performance of my, and André Gide's, *Persephone*. From my conversations with him I felt he had understood my views on the tedious subject, 'music and words'. Not that these views were difficult or obscure, or even original; Beethoven had already expressed them, in sum, in a letter to his publisher: 'Music and words are one and the same thing.' Words combined with music lose some of the rhythmic and sonorous relationships that obtained when they were words only; or, rather, they exchange these relationships for new ones—for, in fact, a new 'music'. They no doubt *mean* the same things; but they are magical as well as meaningful and their magic is transformed when they are combined with music; I do not say that a composer may not try to preserve or imitate effects of purely verbal relationships in music. I have done precisely that myself, in instances where the verse form is strict or where the metre of the verse has suggested a musical construction to me (in the sonnet *Musick to Heare*, for instance). But this approach implies something of what is meant by the phrase 'setting words to music', a limited, pejorative description that is certainly as far from Beethoven's meaning as it is from mine.

Gide understood little or nothing of all this, however; or, if he understood, disagreed. (That Gide understood nothing whatever about music in general is apparent to anyone who has read his *Notes on Chopin*.) He had expected the *Persephone* text to be sung with exactly the same stresses he would use to recite it. He believed my musical purpose should be to imitate or underline the verbal pattern: I would simply have to find pitches for the syllables, since he considered he had already composed the rhythm. The tradition of *poesia per musica* meant nothing to him. And, not understanding that a poet and musician collaborate to produce *one* music, he was only horrified by the discrepancies between my music and his.

I turned to Valéry for support, and no arbiter could have given me more. I do not know what he said to Gide. But to me he affirmed the musician's prerogative to treat loose and formless prosodies (such as Gide's) according to his musical ideas, even if the latter led to 'distortion' of phrasing or to breaking up, for purposes of syllabification, of the words themselves. (But what kind of music did Gide expect of me?)

And when *Persephone* was finally performed, at the end of April 1934, Valéry continued conspicuously to support me by attending all the performances, a fact I much appreciated—especially since his *Semiramis*, produced for the first time only a week after *Persephone*, must have occupied a good deal of his time.

Shortly before the *Persephone première* I composed a statement of my views on the relations of text and music and on the musical syllabification of a text. This manifesto, as it was published in the Paris *Excelsior*, concluded with the words: '. . . a nose is not manufactured: a nose just *is*, thus, too, my art.' After the *première* I received the following letter from Valéry:

The French Academy,
2nd May 1934

My dear Stravinsky, I could not get to you Monday evening to tell you of the extraordinary impression the *Persephone* music made on me. I am only a 'profane listener', but the divine *detachment* of your work touched me. It seems to me that what I have sometimes searched for in the ways of poetry, you pursue and join in your art. The point is, to attain purity through the will. You expressed it marvellously well in the article yesterday which I immensely enjoyed. LONG LIVE YOUR NOSE.

Sincerely yours,
PAUL VALÉRY

Valéry knew little enough about music. But he knew that he knew little and therefore did not utter banalities of the type one so often hears from literary people. He made a point of attending performances of my works, and this touched me. I have a distinct recollection of him at the first presentation of

my *Dumbarton Oaks* Concerto in Paris; my painter son
Theodore made a drawing of him at the time as a present for
me.

*   *   *

The Valéry who most interests me at present is one whose
very existence most critics would deny: the religious. Valéry's
nature *was* in some way religious, no matter how essentially
non-religious his writings. Like Shaw, he had been the friend
of a nun, of several nuns, in fact, and he had had doctrinal
discussions with them. He was not susceptible to any religious orthodoxy, of course, nor, I think, was he even poten-
tially a believer. When he had discovered the fallacy in the
argument that the existence of absolute moral values must
presuppose a Superior Being, when he saw that 'absolute' and
'Superior' represented an analytic contradiction, he did not
look further, and instead of Valéry the theist we have Valéry
the moralist. Nevertheless, he had thoughts that I would call
religious, and these thoughts are revealed in the plays,
especially in *My Faust*. If *Waiting for Godot* is religious, then
so, certainly, is *The Only One*. And the Devil in *Luste* who
says, 'I fell, but I fell from the top,' is the Devil of the Scrip-
tures and no mere personified idea. Valéry is even able to
make this Devil invoke God, as when Mephisto says, 'No one
has ever talked to me like this before. At least . . . not for a
long time.' And Valéry's finest line describing him, 'I am all
the peril that is needed to make a Saint,' is not the line of a
pure moralist; nor is Faust's description of him, 'The Other',
as 'Anything one likes, whatever one likes may be him', nor
Mephisto's own self-description: 'I don't know how to think
and I've got no heart . . . all I know is my job.' Neither did
Valéry in conversation with me display the sceptical temperament for which he was so famous, though in the religious-
literary atmosphere of between-the-wars Paris, with, on the
one hand, Gide and his Protestant manias, and on the other,

77

Claudel and his Wagnerian-Catholic ones, I would have welcomed it.

*   *   *

Valéry is not one of the great innovators of our age, as Joyce was, for example, or Webern, or Klee. He had been altogether too fascinated by the processes of creation. And, he worshipped intellect too much—indeed, to the point of valuing himself more as an intellectual than as a poet. The result of this Teste-ism was his contentment with *epistamenos*, with 'knowing how', at which point he would stop. Valéry's philosophical arguments are more rhetorical than philosophical, in my opinion, even when he is dealing with a pure philosophy such as Descartes's. I am even tempted to assert that Valéry's having written so much about poetry is responsible for dissipating his writing of poetry—though the examples of other poets contradict such an assertion.

I have never *seen* a Valéry play. I am therefore inclined to regard them all as collections of dialogues to be read. (The didactic dialogue on mind in *The Only One* is certainly 'to be read'.) And reading them, I somehow continue to hear all the characters speaking in Valéry's voice. I read, and heard, *My Faust* this way in the last spring of the war, not suspecting, of course, that I would never again hear Valéry's living voice. Very soon after came the news of his death. I grieved for him. His loss was a personal one.

ROMAIN ROLLAND

R.C. How did you come to know Romain Rolland?

I.S. At the beginning of the 1914 war, before the scandal of his *Au dessus de la mêlée*, he wrote asking me to contribute a statement to a book he was then preparing—an indictment of German 'barbarism', I replied as follows:

78

Mon cher confrère! I hasten to answer your appeal for a protest against the barbarism of the German armies. But is 'barbarism' the right word? What is a barbarian? It seems to me that by definition he is someone belonging to a conception of culture new or different from our own; and though this culture might be radically different or antithetical to ours we do not for that reason deny its value, or the possibility that this value might be greater than our own.

But the *present* Germany cannot be considered as a manifestation of 'new culture'. Germany, *as a country*, belongs to the old world and the culture of the country is as old as that of the other nations of Western Europe. However, a nation which in time of peace erects a series of monuments such as those of the Siegesallee in Berlin and which, in time of war, sends her armies to destroy a city like Louvain and a cathedral like Rheims is not barbarian in the proper sense nor civilized in any sense. If 'renewal' is what Germany really seeks, she might better start at home with her Berlin monuments. It is the highest common interest of all those peoples who still feel the need to breathe the air of their ancient culture to put themselves on the side of the enemies of the *present* Germany, and to flee for ever the unbearable spirit of *this* colossal, obese, and morally putrefying Germania.

IGOR STRAVINSKY

P.S. Throughout these terrible days—to which we are the living witnesses—your appeal *L'union fait la force* has been our one encouragement.

Shortly after sending him this letter I made his acquaintance on, of all places, a *lac des quatre Cantons* excursion boat. I was with my wife and children enjoying a day's outing when a tall, spectacled gentleman, evidently doing the same thing, came up to me and shyly introduced himself as my correspondent. I was immediately taken by his personal

charm and intellectual honesty, and though his literature—
Jean-Christophe and *Beethoven the Creator*—were and are
exactly what I most abhor, these books have not obstructed
my feeling for the man.[1] I saw him occasionally after that in
company with Claudel and Jules Romains, if I remember
correctly, at Ramuz's home near Lausanne. Later, he composed an enthusiastic article about *Petroushka* after hearing
it at a concert in Geneva. I wrote to thank him for this
criticism and we became friends.

MANUEL DE FALLA

R.C. What do you remember of Manuel de Falla?

I.S. Sometime in 1910, at Cipa Godebski's, I was introduced to a
man even smaller than myself, and as modest and withdrawn
as an oyster. I took him, Manuel de Falla, for an *homme
sérieux*; in fact, his nature was the most unpityingly religious
I have ever known—and the least sensible to manifestations
of humour. I have never seen anyone as shy. In the course of
a party in his honour following a performance of *El Retablo
de Maese Pedro* at the home of the Princess de Polignac (that
curious American woman who looked like Dante and whose
ambition was to have her bust next to Richelieu's in the
Louvre), it was suddenly noticed that Falla himself had disappeared; he was found sitting alone in the darkened room of
the theatre holding one of Maese Pedro's puppets. I was
always surprised that a man as shy as Falla could bring himself to appear on a stage at all. He did conduct, however, and

[1] Since writing this I have come upon a remark of Rilke's about Rolland
which coincides with my own feelings. Rilke found Rolland a 'sympathetic
personality' (letter of 21st March 1913 to M. von Thurn und Taxis), but
Jean-Christophe was 'indescribably thin, and the scene has been rightly placed
in Germany because of the length and the sentimentality' (letter to the same
of 10th April 1913)—a remark which, by the way, is almost the only attempt
at humour I know of in Rilke.

14. Sketch for the cover of my *Ragtime* by Picasso, 1919

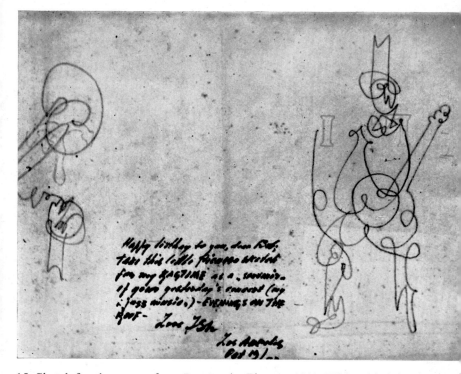

15. Sketch for the cover of my *Ragtime* by Picasso, 1919. With a birthday inscripti
to Robert Craft to whom I gave the drawing after a concert of my 'jazz' music
October 1953. The drawing is one uninterrupted line, beginning with the tail

play the harpsichord—in his concerto, a piece I admire and have conducted myself. In fact, the last time I saw Falla was at a performance of this concerto in London in the 1930s.

Falla was always very attentive to me and my work. When, after the *première* of his *Tricorne*, I told him that the best music in his score was not necessarily the most 'Spanish', I knew my remark would impress him. And he did grow, though his material was so small he could not grow very far. I thought of him as the most devoted of all my musical friends. Whereas, for instance, Ravel turned his back on me after *Mavra*—indeed, the only later work of mine he ever noticed at all was the *Symphony of Psalms*—Falla followed me in all my later music. His ear was very fine, and I think his appreciation was genuine.

REYNALDO HAHN

R.C. Do you have any recollection of Reynaldo Hahn?

S. I saw him quite often, always in company with Marcel Proust. Diaghilev needed him and therefore staged his *Dieu Bleu*; he was the salon idol of Paris, and salon support was very useful to Diaghilev at that time. After the war, however, Diaghilev dropped him for the very reason that he had once found him important—his salon reputation. Hahn was an enthusiast of *Le Sacre du Printemps*, as indeed almost everyone in Paris had become—except for Debussy, who persisted in calling it 'une musique nègre', and the few conservatives, who were calling it 'massacre du Printemps'—and he remained a partisan of my music up to *Pulcinella* which, however, promptly turned him into an enemy. He was a thin, elegant man with motherly manners. Here is a New Year's note from him:

F   *81*

Paris,
1st January 1914

My dear friend, I thank you sincerely for your telegram, and I wish for this year the continuing development of your young glory. I enclose an article of mine that mentions your fascinating personality. You have had in me an admirer 'from the first hour'. But, do not think me a flatterer: I am too pedantic and, I dare say, too meticulous in my feelings to burst without restraint as some do, or to resign myself hypocritically as some others do. I avow my admirations and my true preferences, and I honour whoever is to be honoured. I admire you and esteem you very highly: you are a great musician.

As for my music, I beg of you to think as little good of it as you wish, but believe in my feelings of sincere friendship and profound artistic sympathy.

REYNALDO HAHN

GORODETSKY AND BALMONT[1]

R.C. What do you recollect of the authors of your first song texts, Sergei Gorodetsky and Konstantin Balmont?

I.S. I knew Gorodetsky well in 1906–7 when I was composing the music to his songs. We did not 'collaborate' in them, however, and after hearing them at a concert in St. Petersburg, he confided to me that 'the music is very pretty, but it really does not interpret my texts accurately, since I describe a time-to-time ringing of long, slow bells and your music is a kind of jingle bells'. He was a tall, blond, sickle-nosed man who was later a good friend to my wife Vera in Tiflis during the revolution.

I did not meet Balmont though I saw him at one of our concerts in St. Petersburg: he had bright red hair and goatee,

[1] See *The Poets of Russia 1890–1930* by Renato Poggioli, Harvard, 1960.

82

and he was dead drunk, which was his normal condition from the day of his birth to his death. But I was never close to any Russian literary group, and in fact the only Russian literary intellectuals I ever did know—Merezhkovsky, for instance, and Prince Mirsky—I had met in Paris. Balmont lived in Paris, but I did not encounter him there. His poetry is more significant than Gorodetsky's, and slightly less faded, though as a nature poet, he was easily overshadowed by the revolutionaries, and especially by Alexander Blok. His *Zvezdoliki* ('The Star-Faced One') is obscure as poetry and as mysticism, but its words are good, and words were what I needed, not meanings. I couldn't tell you even now exactly what the poem means.

LORD BERNERS

.C. W hat are your recollections of Lord Berners?

S. I met Gerald Tyrwhitt—he was not yet Lord Berners—in Rome in 1911. He had introduced himself to me as a friend of my St. Petersburg friend Klukovsky. I found him droll and delightful. I saw him often after that and on every trip to Rome during the 1914 war. His remarks about music were perceptive; and though I considered him an amateur, but in the best—literal—sense, I would not call him amateurish, as we now use the word. When we knew each other better, he began to come to me for criticism and advice in his composition. I have often looked through his scores with him at the piano, or listened to them together with him in the theatre, and I thought his *Wedding Bouquet* and his *Neptune* as good as the French works of that kind produced by Diaghilev, though whether or not this could be construed as a compliment I cannot say.

I have already told how Lord Berners aided me when, on my way from Rome to Switzerland in 1917, I was detained by

Italian border police and accused of trying to smuggle a plan of fortifications—in fact, my portrait by Picasso—out of the country. I suddenly thought of Lord Berners because of some Mandorlati figs he had given me to eat on the train; a policeman had confiscated the figs and begun to split them open with his sabre, in search of I know not what contraband. I contacted Berners at the British Embassy, and had the portrait sent to him to be forwarded to me in Switzerland as an official paper.

After the war Berners returned to London. I was a guest of his on each of my English visits. I remember with special pleasure an October weekend in the late 1930s in Faringdon, his country home near Oxford, where one slept in a crystal bed, walked in deep meadows, rode roan horses, and sat by brick fireplaces in Hepplewhite chairs. Faringdon's atmosphere was not exclusively traditional, however. Meals were served in which all the food was of one colour pedigree; i.e., if Lord Berners's mood was pink, lunch might consist of beet soup, lobster, tomatoes, strawberries. And outside, a flock of pink pigeons might fly overhead, for Lord Berners's pigeons were sprayed with (harmless) cosmetic dyes; my wife Vera used to send him saffron dye from France, and a blue powder which he used for making blue mayonnaise.

Lord Berners knew of my interest in old English music and once promised to present me with the complete works of Purcell. I think if he were to visit my home today nothing would please him more than the discovery that my library contains more old English music than any other kind.

Faringdon House,
Berkshire,
9th January 1919

Cher ami, Do you know that I have been bombarding you with letters and post cards from Rome for many months with no result? The Swiss border is a bad joke, and I suppose you have received nothing. In any case, I've had no answer. Meanwhile, however, I saw Carlo Ponti in Paris who gave me news of you. He was full of enthusiasm about the *Ragtime* which you had played him. I was a few days in London, also, where I saw Diaghilev and the Ballet several times. We celebrated the New Year together. I think he will stay in London until March and then go to Monte Carlo. I also saw Lady Cunard and Beecham, who talked about you a great deal. Beecham would like to play *The Nightingale*—has he told you about it? He is always very much in the clouds.

Recently I've written three small pieces for orchestra—*Chinoiserie, Valse sentimentale,* and *Kasatchok*—and they are to be played in Manchester on 8th March. I am pleased about this performance because, for the moment, Manchester has the best orchestra in England and the conductor will do them very well.

I expect to stay in England until March, and then go back to Rome.

Did you know that I had changed my name and am no longer Tyrwhitt? My aunt—or rather my uncle—*à héritage*—died. Unfortunately I inherit only the title, with a lot of taxes to be paid.

I would so much like to see you. I beg you to write me a little note and tell me what you are doing just now.

Your very devoted,
BERNERS

R.C. You must have met many of the Kings and Queens of Europe at gala performances in the early Diaghilev days?

I.S. No, for I contrived to avoid their official courtesies when I could. I do remember a few such confrontations, however, and among these the most impressive was my presentation to Queen Alexandra in her box at Covent Garden after a performance of the *Firebird* in 1912. I had tried to escape this also, but Diaghilev begged me to go, and Lady Ripon promised to be present and to help me. The Queen looked like a birthday cake—she wore a tall wig and was very rosily made up. She smiled at me but said nothing; as she was quite deaf, however, and as this affliction of hers was universally known, any compliment about my music would not have been in order. Most likely the poor woman had not the vaguest notion who I was or what I was doing there.

I knew Alfonso XIII of Spain rather better than this. As a *balletomane* who hardly ever missed a performance of our company in Madrid he often invited Diaghilev and me to his loge. I remember a *soirée* he gave for the dancers and artists of our troupe in some private rooms of the theatre where we were playing. I was seated between Queen Maria and the Queen Mother. I spoke German with the latter, and French with the two sovereigns, though the King himself did not remain at the table but walked about helping to serve us. (Harold Nicolson's description, in *People and Things*, of the solemn annual ceremony in which Alfonso had to wash the feet of a group of beggars gathered from the streets has curiously reminded me of this evening.) Alfonso was a kind man, but he was given to uttering the most awful *sottises*: 'Mon cher, il faut que vous composiez une musique pour les coupoles des églises russes,' which is the sort of remark the Russian Grand Dukes used to make. He wore a medallion portrait of the Emperor Charles V on his chest which invited all who looked at him to compare the family features of the ancestral and the living king.

I also remember being presented to Queen Marie of Rumania, King Carol's mother, the day after a concert in Bucharest in which I played my piano concerto; I think it was in 1925. The Queen had sent me an invitation which my Rumanian friends considered to be indeclinable. Accordingly, I went to the Royal Palace where I was escorted to an ante-room and left in the presence of several ladies-in-waiting, who were very eager to hear about Paris and kept asking me questions. One of them wanted to know what I thought was the most interesting thing in that city. I said the 'marché aux puces' but the word 'puces' seemed to shock them a good deal and they were silent. (I still wonder what *unanständig* meaning that word might have had in Rumanian?) The Queen was both beautiful and a bluestocking: she had been an author herself, like that other Rumanian queen, Carmen Sylva. She was most gracious to me and she even sent me to her bed-room to show me her fine collection of ikons.

But for a few chance meetings and one luncheon with the present Queen Mother of Belgium, who wanted to commission a violin concerto from me, and a brief presentation to the Queen of Holland at The Hague in 1952, these are all the queens of countries I have known.

SOME MUSICAL QUESTIONS

SOME MUSICAL QUESTIONS

'The song people praise is always the latest thing.'
TELEMACHUS, trans. W. H. D. Rouse.

R.C. For whom do you compose?

I.S. For myself and the hypothetical other. Or rather, this is an ideal achieved by only a very few composers. Most of us write for an audience, as, for example, Haydn: '. . . You ask me for an opera buffa. . . . If you intend to produce it on a stage in Prague . . . I cannot comply with your wish because all my operas are far too closely connected with our personal circle (Esterház) and moreover they would not produce the proper effect which I calculated in accordance with the locality.' And, in another letter: 'I have to change many things (in a symphony) for the English public.' But this does not mean that an artist compromises himself when he considers an audience and its tastes. *Hamlet* and *Don Giovanni* were written for real audiences while, at the same time, the authors of these masterpieces had certainly first composed for themselves and the hypothetical other.

PATRONAGE

R.C. Most of your music was composed on commission. Has this circumstance affected the course of your art; that is, have the nature or specifications of a commission ever helped to determine your musical direction, or perhaps imposed a limitation on the musical substance? Would you comment on the role of the commission in contemporary music in general?

I.S. The trick, of course, is to choose one's commission, to compose what one wants to compose and to get it commissioned afterwards, and I myself have had the luck to do this in many instances. But, to reply to your question, I attribute hardly any influence on the direction or the substance of my music to the circumstances of commissions. Though Diaghilev had confronted me with Pergolesi's music, suggesting and finally commissioning me to write a ballet based upon it, and though this circumstance did undoubtedly lead to a new appreciation of eighteenth-century classicism on my part, I consider that I created the possibility of the commission as much as it created me, and that *Pulcinella*, though it may seem to have been an arbitrary step at the time, was an entirely logical step for me.

But, while I minimize the importance of commissions in relation to my own art, I believe that most new music is influenced, and even to some extent predetermined, by them. A certain kind of product *is* expected—however free the terms of a commission may seem to be. For example, a piece of music commissioned for performance by an American symphony orchestra is expected to be performable after four to six hours of rehearsal, to be standard in instrumentation, in length, and, since these standards tend to suggest others, standard in style—i.e., somewhere between Schoenberg and Stravinsky, but domesticated. The composer cannot stray very far from this pattern, e.g., produce a two-minute piece requiring thirty-five hours of rehearsal and twenty extra instruments and written in a style of such originality that the conductor's contract will be cancelled if he plays it. (This particular set of conditions is almost exactly reversed in the major radio stations of West Germany. Funds and rehearsal time for new music are abundant there and—this is my point —the styles of the new music, for better or worse—that is not the point—are, from a performing point of view, of a corresponding complexity.) I do not say that a composer cannot write personal and original music in these conditions; I do say that, inevitably, conditions create patterns.

*   *   *

Probably the most significant difference between the role of the commission today and in the past is the question of utility. Or, at any rate, I imagine that music was commissioned in the past to satisfy an *actual* need. The commissions of a Renaissance Duke, of the Church, of an Esterházy or Diaghilev were of this sort. Actual, i.e., commercial, uses for new music of a high, i.e., non-commercial, quality do still exist, of course—the new concerto for a violinist, the new symphony for the Philharmonic, etc.—but whether the music is really needed for itself and not for some adjunctive value, namely, PUBLICITY, is often difficult to determine. I doubt, for example, that some of the commissioners of my own later music have paid what they have paid just for their musical pleasure. But this is still utility—no matter the motive. In the main, however, the need for new cantatas, string quartets, symphonies, is wholly imaginary, and commissioning organizations, like the Ford and the Rockefeller Foundations, are really only buying up surplus symphonies as the government buys up surplus corn. In fact, the need for such music is so hopelessly non-actual that the commissioners are now obliged to try to buy the need for the symphony as well as the symphony.

Great, i.e., immortal, music creates its own need; whether or not it happened to be commissioned should be a private economic fact of interest only to the composer. Webern's songs with instrumental accompaniment were not commissioned nor did they meet any demand; no performing organization was capable of presenting them at the time they were written. In fact, this music which is so consequential at present is a perpetual embarrassment to the whole idea of commission-for-use. None the less, even Webern could compose music on commission. Thus his *Symphony* for the League of Composers; it probably scandalized the League, and everybody else, but that couldn't have mattered to Webern.

But while the composer is guided by his genius (if he has any, and if he hasn't he doesn't matter), what guides the commissioner? I have just seen a list of composers recently awarded commissions of several thousands of dollars by one of the Foundations. As I know music and, also, some of the music of some of these composers, I think the Foundation concerned would have been wiser and kinder if it had *fined* some of these people the same amount of money, for money will not enrich their music, nor discourage the fulsome ideas of 'success' and 'career' such people pursue and believe to be theirs by the compliments of reviewers who automatically compliment their sort of trash. I have had my own experience with commissioners, too, a brush with Antimaecenas himself—a scion of grocery stores and sciolist of 'modern art'—who would have commissioned *The Rake's Progress* from me, had I agreed to his condition that he should sit in judgment while I played my music to him at the piano.

Do you remember Sigismondo Malatesta's letter to Giovanni di Medici asking for an artist to beautify the newly-plastered walls of the Tempio Malatesta with frescoes? In

Some Musical Questions

Pound's version, Sigismondo wishes to promise the painter, whoever he may be, that he:

> . . . *can work as he likes,*
> *or waste his time as he likes,*
> *never lacking provision.*

That should be read by anyone who intends to commission an artist.

*   *   **

R.C. Has music ever been suggested to you by, or has a musical idea ever occurred to you from, a purely visual experience of movement, line or pattern?

I.S. Countless times, I suppose, though I remember only one instance in which I was aware of such a thing. This was during the composition of the second of my *Three Pieces* for string quartet. I had been fascinated by the movements of Little Tich whom I had seen in London in 1914, and the jerky, spastic movement, the ups and downs, the rhythm—even the mood or joke of the music—which I later called *Eccentric*, was suggested by the art of this great clown (and suggested seems to me the right word, for it does not try to *approfondir* the relationship, whatever it is).

Incidentally, these pieces were not influenced by Schoenberg or Webern, as has been said—at least not to my conscious knowledge. I knew no music by Webern in 1914, and of Schoenberg only *Pierrot lunaire*. But, though my pieces are perhaps thinner in substance and more repetitive than music by Schoenberg and Webern of the same date, they are also very different in spirit, and mark, I think, an important change in my art. In spite of the obvious recollection of *Petroushka* in *Eccentric*, it seems to me these *Three Pieces* look ahead to the *Pièces Faciles* for piano duet of one year later, and from the *Pièces Faciles* to my so aberrant 'neo-classicism' (in which category, nevertheless, and without knowing it was that, I have managed to compose some not unpleasing music).

R.C. How did you happen to use the *Jambe en bois* melody in *Petroushka*?

I.S. A hurdy-gurdy played it every afternoon beneath my window in Beaulieu (near Nice) and since it struck me as a good tune for the scene I was then composing, I wrote it in. I did not think whether the composer might still be living or the music protected by copyright, and Maurice Delage, who was with me, was of the opinion that the 'melody must be very old'. Then, several months after the *première* someone informed Diaghilev that the tune had been composed by a Mr. Spencer, a gentleman still very much alive and resident in France. Since 1911, therefore, a share of *Petroushka*'s royalties has gone to Mr. Spencer or his heirs. I do not cite this to grieve about it, however: I *should* pay for the use of someone else's property. But I do not think it fair that I have to pay, as I must, a sixth of all royalties deriving from purely musical (non-staged) performances of *Petroushka*, even of excerpts, such as the *Russian Dance*, to the co-author of the libretto.[1]

The *Jambe en bois* incident might have had a sequel years

[1] The injustices of copyright laws and non-laws would add a complicated chapter to my 'life' and demand a reinterpretation of some of my composing activity. Those who imagine that my works make me rich do not realize that everything I composed before 1931 (I became a French citizen in 1934, and this citizenship extended authors' rights retrospectively for three years) was and is unprotected in the United States: the United States and the U.S.S.R. failed to sign the Berne copyright convention. I do not receive performance rights for the *Firebird*, which, as one of the most popular pieces of music composed in this century, would have made me a 'millionaire' (though, of course, for the good of my soul, I do not aspire to be any such thing).

The Firebird, Petroushka, and *Le Sacre du Printemps* were pirated in the United States and have been performed there free for the last thirty-five years. I tried to protect the music I composed after these three ballets by having an American editor sign my compositions—a humiliating expedient, though Albert Spalding, who kindly gave his name, was so obviously not a real editor. This stratagem covered only those less frequently performed works of the 1920s, however, which it would not pay a pirate to copy. When I became an American citizen in 1945 I prepared new versions of almost all the music I had composed before 1931. These versions vary from complete re-writings,

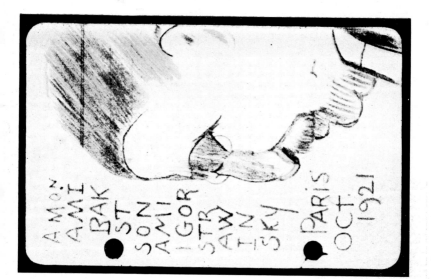

16. (*left*) Diaghilev,
drawn by me, 1921

17. (*right*) Bakst, drawn
by me, 1921

18. Madrid, 1921. Left to right, Robert Delaunay, Boris Kochno, myself, Sonia Delaunay, Diaghilev, Manuel de Falla,

later with the 'Happy Birthday' melody in the *Greeting Pre-lude* I wrote for Pierre Monteux's eightieth birthday (a piece I had already sketched out in 1950 for a project that did not materialize). I must have assumed this melody to be in the category of folk music, too, or, at least, to be very old and dim in origin. As it turned out, the author was alive, but, graciously, did not ask for an indemnity.

R.C. To what extent does your Russian music, especially *Renard* and *Les Noces*, make use of folk melody?

S. There is no conscious use of folk melody whatever in *Renard*, and only one of the themes of *Les Noces* is folk derived; and it is not really a folk melody but a workers'

melody, a proletarian song. This theme, incidentally, was given me by my friend Stepan Mitusov at least ten years before I made use of it in the final tableau of *Les Noces*. Excellent collections of Russian folk music by Tchaikovsky and Liadov, and a more or less good one by Rimsky-Korsakov, had been published; all of these were familiar to me, of course, and while I did not actually turn to folk music as source material, I was undoubtedly influenced by it. The song 'Down St. Peter's Road' in *Petroushka* (St. Petersburg was called simply 'Peter' in the peasant villages—'Are you going

like *Petroushka* and the *Symphonies of Wind Instruments*, to the mere correct-ting of printers' errors—as in the case of the *Capriccio* and *Symphony of Psalms*. But the three popular and lucrative early ballets are still far more commonly played in the old, pirated editions.

I like a story about Schoenberg and an early piece of his that was also unprotected. Someone suggested to him that he change the score, re-write a minim as two tied crotchets, for instance, so that the piece could be copy-righted as a new version. Schoenberg's reply was: 'I can't change anything—it's perfect already.'

G

to Peter?') was taken from Tchaikovsky's collection. There are also three folk melodies in the *Firebird*, the two 'Khorovod' themes

and

and the theme of the *Finale*

which had a dotted rhythm in the original. I do not remember which of the three collections supplied which themes, however.

The opening bassoon melody in *Le Sacre du Printemps* is the only folk melody in that work. It came from an anthology of Lithuanian folk music I found in Warsaw, and not from Borodin or Cui as some critics have suggested; the anthology was a recent publication. And, to my knowledge, none of my Russian songs—*Pribaoutki*, the *Four Russian Peasant Choruses*, the *Four Russian Songs*, the *Berceuses du Chat*— contains folk material. If any of these pieces *sounds* like aboriginal folk music, it may be because my powers of fabrication were able to tap some unconscious 'folk' memory. In each case, however, the syllables and words of the songs dictated the music. The *Balalaika* in my *Pièces Faciles* is also my original melody, like a folk song, of course, but not directly borrowed. One other work of mine, not 'Russian' and therefore not in your category, borrows extensively from folk music. All the themes in my *Norwegian Moods* were taken from a collection of Norwegian folk music my wife had found in a second-hand book store in Los Angeles—and not from Grieg as some writers on my music have stated!

R.C. What prompted you to arrange the *Star-Spangled Banner*?

I.S. I undertook the arrangement at the suggestion of a pupil—a composer, rather, who visited me twice a week to have his works recomposed—and partly because I was obliged to begin my concerts during the war with the *Star-Spangled Banner*, the existing arrangements of which seemed to me very poor. My version was composed in Los Angeles on 4th July 1941, and performed shortly after that by an orchestra and negro chorus conducted by my pupil's son-in-law. After this performance I sent the manuscript to Mrs. F. D. Roosevelt for a war-fund auction, but my major seventh chord in the second strain of the piece, the part patriotic ladies like best, must have embarrassed some high official, for my score was returned with an apology. I then gave it to Klaus Mann, who soon succeeded in selling it for a similar purpose. I performed it myself for the first time with the Boston Symphony Orchestra in the winter of 1944. I stood with my back to the orchestra and conducted the audience, who were supposed to sing but didn't. Though no one seemed to notice that my arrangement differed from the standard offering, the next day, just before the second concert, a Police Commissioner appeared in my dressing-room and informed me of a Massachusetts law forbidding any 'tampering' with national property. He said that policemen had already been instructed to remove my arrangement from the music stands. I argued that if an *Urtext* of the *Star-Spangled Banner* existed, it was certainly infrequently played in Massachusetts—but to no avail. I do not know if my version has been performed since. It ought to be, for it makes the linear and harmonic best of the material, and is certainly superior to any other version I have heard. (The compliment to myself in this comparison is very small indeed.)

ELECTRONIC MUSIC

R.C. Have you any further observations to make about electronic 'music'?

I.S. I would still repeat the criticisms I made of it two years ago —namely, I do not see why a medium so rich in sound possibilities should sound so poor; and, though shape and composition are more in evidence and the liaisons more convincing in the newer pieces, the impression of desultoriness is still a main impression. At the same time the newer electronic music has more direction—a fact I attribute to the clearer division between those who are trying to create a new and purely electronic sound and those who are trying to transform existing sounds, instrumental and otherwise; some attractive results have been attained on both sides of this split. Now, however, with the appearance of the R.C.A. synthesizer the whole electronic music experiment up to the present can only be regarded as a pre-natal stage in its development.

Also, many composers have now begun to see a use for electronically produced sound, mixed or used adjunctively with traditional instrumental sound—though no one, I think, has been entirely successful in bridging the modulatory ground between the two. I myself am interested in this problem of bringing together the live and the mechanical. In fact, my first idea, in 1917, for the instrumentation of *Les Noces* was to use mechanical instruments, player pianos, together with ordinary orchestral instruments—an idea I abandoned only because I did not know how to co-ordinate and control both elements.

Perhaps the real future of electronic music is in the theatre. Imagine the ghost scene in *Hamlet* with electronic 'white noise' entering the auditorium from several directions (Berio's *Omaggio à Joyce* is perhaps a preview of this kind of thing). But this very theatricality—which electronicians will object to as more for the effect of another art than for the thing itself—exposes another problem. 'Concerts' of electronic music are, in fact, more like séances. With nothing to look at on the stage—no exhibition of orchestra and conductor, but only conduit-speaker boxes and, suspended from the ceiling, mobile reflectors—what is the audience to look at? Surely not at anything so arbitrary as the 'symbolic' colours and pictures of the San Francisco 'Vortex' experiment?

I have uncovered a Diaghilev letter that should be of at least historical interest in the discussion of 'Futuristic' music, *musique concrète*, and electronic music. It is dated Rome, 8th March 1915, and was sent to me at the Hotel Victoria, Château d'Oex, Switzerland. It is naïve, of course, but not more so than the 'Futuristic' composers themselves; and, it is a good example of Diaghilev's flair.

'. . . now to something else, and much more important. An idea of genius has come to my mind. After having thirty-two rehearsals of the *Liturgie*, we have concluded that absolute silence is death . . . and that aerial space is not absolute silence and cannot be. Silence doesn't exist and couldn't exist. Therefore, dance action must be supported not by music but by sounds, *id est*, by filling the ear harmonically. The source of this 'filling' should not be recognizable. The changes of these harmonic junctures, or liaisons, must not be remarked by the ear—one sound merely joins or enters another, *id est*, there is no obvious rhythm whatsoever, because one does not hear either the beginning or the end of the sound. The projected instruments are: bells wrapped round with cloth and other material, aeolian harps, guzli,[1] sirens, tops, and so on. Of course all this has to be worked out, but for that purpose Marinetti proposes we get together for some days in Milan and discuss it with the leader of their 'orchestra', and examine all their instruments. Also, he guarantees that at this time he will bring Pratella to Milan so he can show us his newest works which are, according to him, *formidables*. We could do it between the 15th and 20th of March.

Telephone me at Naples, Hotel Vesuvio, if you can come to meet us in Milan. You will see many new Futuristic studios; from there we will go together to Montreux. I urge you very strongly to come—it is very important for the future. I will send you some money for the trip immediately. As for the concert of Prokofiev in Geneva, he can give it as a benefit for the Serbs if he is busy on the 20th. Then, until we meet soon,

je t'embrasse,

SERIOSHA

P.S. Compose *Noces* quickly. I am in love with it.

VARÈSE

R.C. Some of this might be a description of the music of Edgar Varèse? What do you make of Varèse?

I.S. There is nobility in his noise and he himself is a noble figure in our music (how much more honest to have kept his long silence than to have written the apish music of so many

---

[1] The goat plays this instrument in *Renard*.

others). And it is useless to remark, as many do, that his music is limited and repetitive, and that after he had done the one kind of thing he had nowhere to go. The point is he *had* done the one thing. I have never heard *Amériques* and *Arcana* (they *look* as though the shadow of *Le Sacre* had fallen over them), but I do know and greatly admire *Ionisation, Octandre, Density 21. 5,* and *Intégrales,* and I consider Varèse's present activity—tape recording the sound of New York City—of the highest value and not merely as documentation, but as material of art.

WEBERN

.C. Have you changed your mind in any particular about Webern?

S. No; he is the discoverer of a new distance between the musical object and ourselves and, therefore, of a new measure of musical time; as such he is supremely important. But Webern's importance is now recognized even by the matinée idols. A celebrated conductor who recently performed one of the two pieces by him that could be called popular conceded in an interview that 'Webern does have an influence on music', a statement comparable in politics to Eisenhower's discovering communists in China.

Webern the man has now begun to emerge, too, with the publication of his letters to Berg, Humplik, and Jone. The Webern of the letters is, first of all, profoundly religious, and not only institutionally (extraordinary, though, that he should compare the six movements of his second cantata to a Kyrie, a Gloria, a Credo, a Benedictus, a Sanctus, an Agnus Dei), but in the simple holiness of his feeling towards each of God's *essents* (a flower, a mountain, 'silence') as well. Music is a mystery to him, a mystery he does not seek to explain. At the same time, no other meaning exists for him but music,

103

He stands before the Parthenon friezes and marvels at the sculptor's 'conception' which he compares to his own 'composition method . . . always the same thing in a thousand different ways' (in another letter: '. . . the meaning is always the same however different the means'). He never explains beyond that, and he even admits, in one letter, to being severely tried by the necessity of explanation: 'I am sometimes . . . tortured by teaching.'

He is like a village priest in that his world does not extend beyond his village—indeed, he makes *my* world seem a million miles away. His manners and address are also both *villageoises* and . . . priestly. He contains no word of technical jargon (to Berg: 'art must be simple') and no aesthetics ('I don't understand what "classic" and "romantic" mean'). He is infinitely patient and, of course, he takes infinite pains[1] but composing is entirely natural to him. He does not have a rebellious heart—indeed, he accepts without criticism the musical tradition to which he was born—nor has he any conception of himself as a radical composer; he was what he was wholly apart from the so-called *Zeitgeist*. This Webern will embarrass 'Webernists'. They will blush for their master's 'naïvety' and 'provincialism'. They will cover his nakedness and look the other way. And this turning away will coincide, too, with a reaction against his music (in favour of Berg's; I hear everywhere now that Webern's series are too symmetrical, that his music makes one too conscious of twelves, that *la structure sérielle chez Berg est plus cachée*; for me, however, Berg's music, compared with Webern's, is like an old woman about whom one says 'how beautiful she must have been when she was young'). Webern was too original—i.e.,

---

[1] That his music cost him terrible birth pains I have no doubt. The few musical examples in the letters indicate how deeply he had been concerned in his later music with the relation of note values to musical substance (and tempo, metre, beat), and how this problem alone involved him in several stages of re-writing.

too purely himself. Of course the entire world had to imitate him, of course it would fail, of course it will blame Webern. No matter, though. The desperate contrivance of most of the music now being charged to his name can neither diminish his strength nor stale his perfection. He is a perpetual Pentecost for all who believe in music.

*   *   *

.C. Would you analyse your own composing process in any part of one of your more recent pieces—in, for example, the little *Epitaphium*?

S. I began the *Epitaphium* with the flute-clarinet duet (which I had originally thought of as a duet for two flutes and which can be played by two flutes; the piece was written to be performed in a programme with Webern's songs, op. 15, which use the flute-clarinet combination). In the manner I have described in our previous conversations I heard and composed a melodic-harmonic phrase. I certainly did not (and never do) begin with a purely serial idea and, in fact, when I began I did not know, or care, whether all twelve notes would be used. After I had written about half the first phrase I saw its serial pattern, however, and then perhaps I began to work towards that pattern. The constructive problem that first attracted me in the two-part counterpoint of the first phrase was the harmonic one of minor seconds. The flute-clarinet responses are mostly seconds, and so are the harp responses, though the harp part is sometimes complicated by the addition of third, fourth, and fifth harmonic voices. (The harp in this piece, as in all my music, must be pinched *près de la table* to produce the sound I want; incidentally, the deep bass notes of the harp are, I think, the most beautiful on the instrument.)

Only after I had written this little twelve-note duet did I conceive the idea of a series of funeral responses between bass and treble instruments and, as I wanted the whole piece to be very muffled, I decided that the bass instrument should be a harp. The first bar of the harp part was, however, written last. As I worked the music out, it became a kind of hymn, like Purcell's *Funeral Music for Queen Mary*. There are four short antiphonal strophes for the harp, and four for the wind duet, and each strophe is a complete order of the series— harp: O, I, R, RI; winds: O, RI, R, I.

*   *   *

I *have* discovered new (to me) serial combinations in the *Movements* for piano and orchestra, however (and I have discovered in the process, too, that I am becoming not less but more of a serial composer; those younger colleagues who already regard 'serial' as an indecent word, in their claim to have exhausted all that is meant by it and to have gone far beyond, are, I think greatly in error); and the *Movements* are the most advanced music from the point of view of construction of anything I have composed. No theorist could determine the spelling of the note order in, for example, the flute solo near the beginning or the derivation of the three F's announcing the last movement simply by knowing the original order, however unique the combinatorial properties of this particular series. Every aspect of the composition was guided by serial forms, the sixes, quadrilaterals, triangles, etc. The fifth movement, for instance (which cost me a gigantic effort—I rewrote it twice), uses a construction of twelve verticals. Five orders are rotated instead of four, with six alternates for each of the five, while at the same time, the six 'work' in all directions, as though through a crystal.

Now that I have mentioned my new work I should say, too, that its rhythmic language is also the most advanced I have so far employed; perhaps some listeners might even

detect a hint of serialism in it, too. My polyrhythmic combinations are meant to be heard vertically, however, unlike
those of some of my colleagues. Though parallels are not
equivalents, look at Josquin for a parallel, that marvellous
second *Agnus Dei* (the three-voice one) in the *Missa l'Homme
armé*, or at Baude Cordier's *pour le deffault du dieu Bacchus*,[1]
or, for even more remarkable examples, at the Cyprus
Codex.

Each section of the piece is confined to a certain range of
instrumental timbre (another suggestion of serialism?), but
the movements are related more by tempo than by contrasts
of such things as timbre, 'mood', character; in a span of only
twelve minutes, the contrast of an *andante* with an *allegro*
would make little sense; construction must replace contrast.
Perhaps the most significant development in the *Movements*,
however, is their tendency towards anti-tonality—in spite of
long pedal-point passages such as the C of the first ending,
the clarinet trill at the end of the third movement, and the
string harmonies in the fourth movement. I am amazed at
this myself, in view of the fact that in *Threni* simple triadic
references occur in every bar.

Pour le :—— def [fault]

FILM MUSIC AND FILMS

R.C. Have you ever considered writing music for films?

I.S. Yes, several times, and in two instances I had even begun to compose, not 'film music', which is aural erethism, an emotional counterpart to scenery, but music for film use; my *Four Norwegian Moods* were originally intended for a film about the Nazi invasion of Norway, and my *Scherzo à la Russe* began as music for another war film, with a Russian setting. Neither score differed in any way from its present concert form, however, though I re-orchestrated the *Scherzo* for the Paul Whiteman band later; I could conceive of music for films only as incidental music, which is what these pieces are. That this conception is quite wrong from the film industry's point of view I am well aware, but it is as far as I will go, and I can probably count myself fortunate that none of the proposals Hollywood has made me ever reached a contractual stage.

I do enjoy negotiating with film people, though, for only rarely do they try to obscure their motives with nonsense about art. They want my name, not my music—I was even offered $100,000 to pad a film with music, and when I refused, was told that I could receive the same money if I were willing to allow someone else to compose the music in my name. The classical Hollywood story is not mine but Schoenberg's, however. The great composer, who earned almost nothing from his compositions, was invited to supply music for *The Good Earth*, at a fee that must have seemed like Croesus's fortune to him, but with impossible artistic conditions attached. He refused, saying, 'You kill me to keep me from starving to death.' Incidentally, Schoenberg's *Accompaniment to a Cinematograph Scene* is by far the best piece of real film music ever written, an ironic triumph if there ever were one, for the film itself was imaginary.

Some Musical Questions

I first saw a moving picture in St. Petersburg in 1904. (I am certain of the date as it was shortly after Tchekov's death, an event that impressed me, though the fact of his illness was well known, and though I was never a great admirer of his—to my taste—too intellectualized literature.) I remember waiting a long while in a small, crowded room and then seeing a film that proved to be an advertisement for Swiss chocolate. A woman stood by a table pouring hot chocolate into a cup, and a child then swallowed the contents of the cup. That was all. The whole performance lasted no longer than a Bagatelle by Webern, and the cup and the liquid trembled terribly. A second short film was shown, too, a conflagration in a Swedish match factory.

My real interest in films began in 1912 with the first Chaplins—at any rate, I seem to remember seeing a Chaplin film then, in Nice, in company with Michel Larionov, but if that is not accurate I am positive I saw a Chaplin film with Diaghilev in Santander, in 1915. I also remember *Les Mystères de New York*, in Lausanne, I think in 1912. This was one of the first of the 'to be continued next week' serialized adventures, and though it was the most shameless *chyepouha*, the insidious secret of films is such that I was there again each next week.

Chaplin was an event in my life, as he was in Diaghilev's. His so prodigal inventiveness was a continual amazement to me; but I was touched also by the moral point of each Chaplin episode, as well as by the moral of the whole film. (For example, the lunch scene on the tempest-driven boat where he tries to impale a single *petit pois* rolling about his plate like the ball in a pin machine. The Chaplin touch is in the moral ending: when finally he picks up the pea with his fingers, a lady looks on in disgust.) I met Chaplin in Hollywood in 1937 and we became friends. I had concerts there at the time, and he came with me to my rehearsals. For me, Chaplin *is* Hollywood, in its brief age of art.

Film music is significant, in many ways, of course, but not as music, which is why the proposition that better composers could produce better film music is not necessarily true: the standards of the category defeat higher standards. Still, I must express my respect for the craftsmanship of the many good musicians employed by the films, especially the arrangers, who are often responsible for more than the word 'arranger' would seem to imply; in fact, it is said that in Hollywood Haydn would have been credited as the composer of the *Variations on a theme by Haydn* and Brahms as their 'arranger'.

*   *   *

'*Teaching makes of art a virtue.*'

THE LORD OF SUGAWARA

(in the Bunraku play by Chikamatsu)

R.C. Why did you never become a teacher?

I.S. I have very little gift for teaching, and no disposition for it: I am inclined to think that the only pupils worth having would become composers with or without my help (though I am not sure that I would say the same thing in the same way about Berg and Webern in relation to Schoenberg). My instinct is to recompose, and not only students' works, but old masters' as well. When composers show me their music for criticism all I can say is that I would have written it quite differently. Whatever interests me, whatever I love, I wish to make my own (I am probably describing a rare form of kleptomania). I regret my inability, however, and I am full of veneration for Hindemith, Krenek, Sessions, Messiaen, and those few other composers who possess the teacher's gift.

R.C. Your remarks about 'virtuosi' (in the first volume of our 'conversations') might easily be misunderstood. Would you describe the kind of performer you mean?

I.S. I mean, of course, the false virtuosi, the virtuosi without *virtù*, for the term is no longer prestigious; but I should have distinguished between past and present examples, and in the present between the true and the false. Whereas the virtuosi of other eras collaborated closely with new music in exploring new instrumental possibilities and extending technique, the virtuosi of today are inclined to pronounce the most interesting new music—no matter how often 'lesser' performers play it—unplayable. But true virtuosi do still exist. They are the exceptional instrumentalists—the flute player in Rome (Gazzelloni), the clarinettist in Paris (Deplus), and others, who really have attained new instrumental and musical powers through their performances of new music. They are unknown, of course, but their value to music is greater than that of their famous colleagues.

I would define the false virtuoso as that performer who plays only nineteenth-century music, even when it is by Bach and Mozart; or, as the kind of performer who should begin his recitals with the encores, since they are what he plays best.

PERFORMANCE AND INTERPRETATION

R.C. Would you comment on any recent performances of Haydn, Mozart, or Beethoven you may have heard?

I.S. A few days ago I was exposed to a Toscanini recording of Beethoven's first symphony. The *Adagio molto* introduction was played not adagio but andante, in an undivided beat of four and badly played from the very first chord which was not unanimous. The *Allegro* was also an absurdly fast Rossini-like tempo that obliterated phrase accents and articulations, except in the little G minor episode ('cellos, basses and oboe), where even Toscanini must have sensed something wrong—for a moment his pace slackened almost to the right tempo. And Toscanini's ambition throughout the movement seems to have been to create climaxes, whether or not they coincided with Beethoven's own climaxes and, especially, Beethoven's own scale of climax. The second movement was also badly played. At one place in the development section the strings performed strict demisemiquavers after dotted notes. Then, a few bars later, the winds doubly shortened these demisemiquavers (as indeed they were right so to do).[1] The strings hearing themselves corrected followed suit in the next statement of this rhythm. But can Toscanini have failed to hear such a thing? In any case, he did not hear that the ritardando he applied to the beginning of the recapitulation was insufferably gross, that the whole minuet and trio were so absurdly fast as to make no sense at all, and that the last movement was not only too fast but too slick as well, so that the finest passage in the symphony—the dozen bars or so which open the development (bars 96–108)—was reduced to insignificance.

I am not a *doryphore*, nor have I grievances against Toscanini other than those just stated. I submit, however, that these remarks are the sort that music critics should make about Toscanini's or anybody else's performance of Beethoven's first symphony; and, until they (the critics) are able to discern such realities of musical performance ('discern' and 'criticize' have the same root, by the way) they have no right to utter the hieratic nonsense about interpretation they do in fact utter.

Two weeks ago I witnessed a concert of three symphonies, one by Haydn, from the first Salomon series, Mozart's A major (K. 201), and Beethoven's second. I love the Haydn for the different lengths of its sentences, but it was stifled by

---

[1] On the other hand, Beethoven's seventh symphony has been ruined by shortening both the dot and the subsequent note in every performance I have heard:

♩．♫♩　♩．♫♩　　soon becomes　　♪．♫♩　♪．♫♩

19. Cocteau, Picasso, myself, Olga Picasso, Antibes, 1926

20. Myself, Prokofiev, Pierre Souvtchinsky, at Talloires (Lac d'Annecy), 1929
composed my *Capriccio* in this two-room prefabricated summer house. Pierre Sou
chinsky, the Russian philosopher and music critic, was one of my closest frie
between 1920 and 1939, and again in recent years. He was also a tenor, and once sa
the role of Oedipus in my *Oedipus Rex* in Barcelona. Souvtchinsky was present at
first performance of the *Scherzo Fantastique* (he remembers my aunt coming up to
afterwards to say, not, as I expected, 'Congratulations', but 'How is Mama?'),
Fireworks (he says there were cries of 'author' after it and that I appeared on st
walking very rapidly and holding my fur hat in my hand), and of the St. Petersb
première (in the autumn of 1913) of *Le Sacre du Printemps*

tempi too fast and too slow—the *Andante* was played adagio
and both allegros were played prestissimo: the natural respi-
ration of the music was everywhere frustrated and the performance was unreal—pulsation is the reality of music. Next
day, however, the reviewers' only comment was that the
strings had sounded like 'velvet'—though Haydn's strings
should sound like strings and not like velvet. But the word
'interpretation' was saved for the Mozart. Now, the interpre-
tative ground of this little symphony is (*a*) beat: the first
movement should be in cut, i.e., 2/2 time and the last movement in 3/8, the bars divided in half; and, (*b*) style. That is all
the interpretation possible; the word is a myth. But the really
extraordinary event of the concert was the introduction to
the Beethoven, for the conductor gave the first note of the
symphony, the demisemiquaver, as a down-beat. His purpose,
of course, was to make the orchestra attack together, but the
character of the second note, and, indeed, of the whole introduction was thereby destroyed. One preparatory up-beat is
enough to accomplish a clean attack, but, as this conductor's
beat was like hot plasticine, he naturally could not, by a
simple motion, cause the whole orchestra to feel a sub-
division of demisemiquavers. Concerning this, however, the
reviewers said nothing.

*   *   *

R.C. What is academicism in music?

S. Academicism results when the reasons for the rule change,
but not the rule; the academic composer is therefore concerned more with the old rule than with the new reality—
though by 'rule' I mean something nearer to 'principle'; a
rule, in the simple sense, is a mere means of conformity in an
imitative exercise.

If the real end of academicism is knowledge itself, as I
think it is, then, academically speaking, I know very little.

Though I have worked all my life in sound, from an academic point of view I do not even know what sound is (I once tried to read Rayleigh's *Theory of Sound* but was unable mathematically to follow its simplest explanations). My knowledge is activity. I discover it as I work, and I know it while I am discovering it, but only in a very different way before and after.

R.C. How do you think the development of information theory in music might affect your art?

I.S. I have always been interested in the theory of games (since a childhood reading of Cardano, in fact) but this has not meant anything to me as a composer or even helped me at Las Vegas. I realize that choice is an exact mathematical concept, and that I ought to be looking beyond the particular example for the process that generated it (even though the particular example is all that matters to me). I realize, too, that a really comprehensive information theory can explain 'inspiration'—or, anyway, the equation of its components— and, indeed, almost everything else about my processes of musical communication. But though I am confident these explanations would enlighten me, I am even more confident they would not help me to compose. My attitude is merely proof that I am not an intellectual, and therefore problems of explanation are of no very great interest to me. To borrow G. E. Moore's example—'I do not see how you can explain to anyone who does not already know it, what "yellow" is'— I do not see any means of explaining why I have chosen a certain note if whoever hears it does not already know why when he hears it.

R.C. What does 'creation' mean to you?

I.S. Nothing. The word was already badly overloaded when psychologists made it their propaganda term for what was no more than a change in methodology: a child's scribble is not an 'act of creation', nor is our intestinal function, as Freud thought, since animals do as much and animals cannot create; the word, which to Coleridge meant the noblest operation of imagination, is now horribly debased. Only God can create.

.C. And 'modern'?

S. The only sense in which I think 'modern' can now be used must derive from, or so I imagine, a meaning similar to that of the *devotio moderna* of Thomas à Kempis. It implies a new fervour, a new emotion, a new feeling. It is 'romantic', of course, and it suffers (*paschein*, to suffer, is also the root of pathos, incidentally) for it cannot accept the world as it is. 'Modern' in this sense does not so much mean or emphasize the appearance of a new style though, of course, a new style is part of it. Nor is it brought about merely by its innovations, though innovations are part of it too.

This is very far from the popular association of the word with all that is newest and most shocking in the world of sophisticated unmorality. I was once introduced to someone at a party with the recommendation, 'Son *Sacre du Printemps* est terriblement moderne', 'terriblement' meant 'terribly good', of course. And Schoenberg's *bon mot*, 'my music is not modern, it is just badly played', depends on the same popular association of the word, though Schoenberg himself, according to my meaning, is a true, archetypal 'modern'.

CHROMATICISM

.C. You often associate 'pathos' with chromaticism. Do you really believe in an innate connection?

S. Of course not; the association is entirely due to conventions, like those of *musica riservata*; artists believe not in innate qualities but in art. Nevertheless, 'chromatic' and 'pathos' are connected, and the first musical use of chromatic, in the *misura cromatica*, was meant to indicate a rhythmic change for expressive, i.e., pathetic, purposes. I prefer to use chromatic in a limited sense, and in relation to diatonic. But we have acquired the habit of looking for *our* (post-Wagnerian) chromaticism in old music, with the result that contexts are grossly distorted. For example, in his setting of the funeral sentence *In the midst of Life we are in Death*, at the words 'Art justly displeased', Purcell avoids the conventional cadence and composes one that was certainly intended, in one sense, to displease his audience; but the cadence pleases *us* in another sense, far more than the conventional one would have done. In fact, though, our whole approach to sixteenth-century music is apt to be slanted towards a chromaticism that was really no more than a tiny development. Willaert's *Quid Non Ebrietas* quartet,[1] though it is not so much chromatic as modulatory, was the only work of its kind by Willaert (how I would like to have known Willaert, this little man—you remember Calmo's description—who restored Venice to its musical glory), and so were Lasso's *Alma Nemes* and Hans Leo Hassler's *Ad Dominum Cum Tribularer* unique chromatic works by these masters. And, though I do not know music by Stefano Rossetti and Matthias Greiter other than the chromatic pieces Lowinsky has printed, the fact that only these pieces have gained attention proves my point.

*   *   *

Incidentally, I should like to hear someone learned in both sixteenth and seventeenth century music discuss a notion of mine, based roughly on a few examples, that the century of chromatic development from Clemens non Papa through Rore and Wert to Marco da Gagliano, Luzzaschi, Macque (the beautiful seconda Stravaganza), and Gesualdo, etc.,

---

[1] Thanks to Professor Lowinsky it need no longer be called the 'Chromatic Duo'.

exceeds in sureness of harmonic movement and in the use of dissonance the chromaticism of the operatic composers of the seventeenth century—always excepting Purcell. In fact, not until Bach do we find music as advanced, in our sense—the Bach of the chorale preludes and, if he wrote it, of the *Kleines harmonisches Labyrinth*—as the motets and madrigals of the late sixteenth-century masters.

*   *   *

But we cannot experience the full power of Gesualdo's or any sixteenth-century master's chromatic expression precisely because we are unable to hear it contrasted with the customary diatonic music which was its background (and because our ears have been corrupted by later music). Huizinga remarks the greater contrasts of all things in the late Middle Ages, and though his period is earlier than ours, the contrast between chromatic and diatonic might be added to his list. '. . . Illness and health presented a more striking contrast; the cold and darkness of winter were more real evils. Honours and riches were . . . contrasted more vividly with surrounding misery. . . . The contrast between silence and sound, darkness and light, like that between summer and winter, was more strongly marked than it is in our lives. The modern town hardly knows silence or darkness in their purity, nor the effect of a solitary light or a single distant cry.'

'Chromaticism' means something different to each and every composer today.

*   *   *

R.C. You often say you cannot 'think' about composing before you actually start work.

I.S. I do not try to 'think' in advance—I can only start to work and hope to leap a little in my spirit.

Some Musical Questions

R.C. What piece of new music has most interested you in the last year?

I.S. Stockhausen's *Gruppen*. The title is exact: the music really does consist of groups, and each group is admirably composed according to its plan of volume, instrumentation, rhythmic pattern, tessitura, dynamic, various kinds of highs and lows (though perhaps the constant fluctuation of highs and lows, a feature of this kind of music, is its very source of monotony). Also, the music as a whole has a greater sense of movement than any of Stockhausen's other pieces (I have not yet heard *Zyklus*[1]), though I do not think the form is more successful than that of the *Zeitmasse*. Historically, I suppose, the chief significance of *Gruppen* is in its post-serial inventions, but as my own chief interest in music is still note-against-note counterpoint, and as Stockhausen's is in pattern and shape, I may be excused for remarking the exterior aspects.

The question of the three orchestras has aroused much comment. Actually, when the orchestras play separately or overlap, their roles are very marked, but in the tutti sections they simply sound like one orchestra, and this is true of all poly-orchestral music whether it is by Schütz or Mozart or Charles Ives, or anyone else. (It may not be true of Stockhausen's new *Carree*, however.)

The problem of the three conductors is more complicated. If I were to blindfold three conductors and start them beating 60 to a beat, they would not be together at the end of even ten bars. Therefore, when the metronomic indication for one orchestra is 70, for the second 113.5, and for the third 94, these tempi are unattainable with any exactitude by merely human conductors. What, in fact, happens is that the con-

---

[1] The score of which is very Cage-y, though very attractive to look at, too—one almost wishes it didn't have to be *translated* into sound but were a kind of hand-drawn photo-electric sound (after a spectrum).

118

ductors follow each other, juggle, and adjust. Incidentally, this is also why I would rather listen to than conduct one of the orchestras in *Gruppen*: the business of synchronizing with the other conductors and of concentrating on the details of one's own orchestra makes the whole very difficult to hear.

Stockhausen's orchestra is full of remarkable sounds. Let me cite only a few places: the 'cello and bass music at bar 16, for example; the solo guitar music at bar 75, and the music three bars before bar 102. But perhaps the most exciting sounds in the whole score are near the beginning—the pizzicato third orchestra at bar 27, the third orchestra at bars 63 to 68, and especially the brass trills and fluttertongues at bars 108 to 116.

The rhythmic construction of *Gruppen* is, I think, of the greatest interest. For example, the following bar,[1]

<hr>

[1] The musical example is used by permission of Universal Edition, Vienna, the copyright owners.

which means that without showing the actual rhythmic relation of the notes they should sound in this order:

R.C. Does the orchestral player or chorus singer in certain types of new music understand his own role in the composition? For instance, when he plays one of the parts in the bar from Stockhausen's *Gruppen* you have quoted, is he not performing a merely mechanical job which, in fact, a mechanical agent might perform better?

I.S. Just how much do you think the choral singer understood of his 'role' in the structure and composition of, say, the fourteenth-century motets in Dr. Apel's collection? Much new music does appear to contain a large mechanical element, of course, but whether or not the effort to perform it is mechanical depends on the performer and his experience.

For example, I have heard several performances of Webern's *Variations for Orchestra* in the last few years but I have never been able to answer those critics of it who maintained that the players were unable to understand the inter-relationships of their roles without the score. Recently, however, at a rehearsal of that work in Hamburg I actually did observe musicians listening to each other, and not only for the line of the music but for its every nuance as well. The conductor, therefore, ceased to be the usual puppeteer and became a kind of monitor in a large work of co-operation.

At the same time, a purely mechanical element does exist in music today and it might be better if it were isolated and relegated to mechanical means. I am in sympathy with Milton Babbitt when he says that he is 'depressed by the sight of

duplicative'—Mr. Babbitt has his own vocabulary— 'orchestral musicians'.

.C. Is any musical element still susceptible to radical exploitation
and development?

S. Yes, pitch. I even risk a prediction that pitch will comprise
the main difference between the 'music of the future' and our
music, and I consider that the most important aspect of
electronic music is the fact that it can manufacture pitch. Our
mid-twentieth century situation, in regard to pitch, might
perhaps be compared to that of the mid-sixteenth century,
when, after Willaert and others had proved the necessity of
equal temperament, the great pitch experiments began—
Zarlino's quarter-tone instrument, Vincentino's thirty-nine-
tones-to-the-octave archicembalo, and others. These instruments failed, of course, and the well-tempered clavier was
established (though at least three hundred years before Bach),
but our ears are more ready for such experiments now—mine
are at any rate. I had been watching the Kuramatengu play in
Osaka one afternoon recently and had become accustomed to
the Noh flute. Later, in a restaurant, I suddenly heard an
ordinary flute playing ordinary (well-tempered) music. I was
shocked, music apart—I think I could keep the music apart
anyway—by the exprive poverty of the *tuning*.

1912—AND AFTER

R.C. Do you see any similarities between the present (post-war)
years of musical 'exploration' and 'revolution' and the era
before the first world war; and, if so, do you then foresee a
decline from this 'radical exploratory' movement—a decline
into formulation, such as the late 1920s and 1930s might be
considered to have been in relation to the pre-war years?

.S. I can hardly assess a development to which I myself am still contributing, but the richest musical years in this century do now seem to have been those immediately before the 1914 war, and, specifically, 1912, for to that date belong *Pierrot lunaire, Jeux*, the *Altenberg Lieder*, and *Le Sacre du Printemps*.[1]

The stage following the summit of 1912 was also wonderfully rich and even more protean, though it could be considered something of a decline in originality and explosive force, at least from *Le Sacre* and *Pierrot*. Webern's songs with instruments belong to this period, and so does *Wozzeck*, and Schoenberg's *Serenade* and *Five Pieces*, op. 23, and my own *Renard, Noces, Soldat*, and the *Symphonies of Wind Instruments*. This is still the period of exploration and discovery, however. Your so-called period of formulation came only in the later 1920s, with the establishment of so-called 'neo-classicism'—Schoenberg's, Hindemith's, and my own. During the fifteen years from 1930 to 1945, however, these three 'neo-classic' schools were ascendant and the fact that they can be called schools is already an indication of the onset of formulae. The Schoenberg, or, as it is now called, the dodecaphonic school, for all its great merits, was obsessed by an artificial need to abnegate any suggestion of triadic 'tonality'—a very difficult thing to do. And, curiously, its music

---

[1] *Le Sacre du Printemps* is usually dated 1913 but it was completed a full year before its performance.

The *Altenberg*, or *Ansichtskarten Lieder*, though still relatively unknown, are one of the perfect works composed in this century and worthy of comparison with any music by Webern or Schoenberg up to the same date. Incidentally, they seem to me to approach Webern very closely in form, instrumentation and, despite their Wagnerism, sensibility. What exquisite pieces they are, especially the Passacaglia . . . 'Hier tropft Schnee leise in Wasserlachen. . . .'

Since I have already expressed my reservations about *Jeux*—I consider the musical substance too poor for the musical working-out—perhaps I should now say why I value it. *Jeux* discovers a whole new world of nuance and fluidity. These qualities are French, even peculiarly French perhaps, but they are new. The work's influence on Boulez is therefore natural (and natural too is its lack of influence on me, for its free-beat, loose bar-lines are worlds apart from my rarely-rubato, strong-bar-line music). I would still call *Jeux* decadent, though I mean that only in relation to my own development.

was heavily founded in the most turgid and graceless Brahms.

As for my imitators, my 'school' if you prefer, their trouble was that they imitated not so much my music as my person in my music. They were noted for their rhythms, their ostinatos, their 'unexpected' accents, their diatonic 'lines', their 'dissonances', and for their final C major chords with B natural or A in them. The characteristics of the Hindemith school were its interminable 9/8 movements, its endless fourths and its fugues with subjects thirty-two bars long. Other schools existed, of course—the Broadway, the Appalachian, the Neo-Neanderthal (Orff), the *arrière-garde*, etc.—but these three were principal and paramount.

All three schools had come to a stalemate, however, when at the end of the war in 1945 a new period of exploration and revolution began precisely with the rediscovery of the masterpieces of 1912, and the music of Webern in general. Boulez's cantatas are representative of this new music of the immediate post-war. They derive from the Webern cantatas in substance and style but are more complex in texture. (In fact, with them the ideal of a thin, neo-classic line disappears.) In this new period of exploration the only significant work so far is Boulez's *Le Marteau sans maître* (1954).

The next work in this succession, it is already apparent, must utilize musico-electronic means, exploit acoustical mirror effects, and mix composed with improvised elements. But enough of soothsaying: I am a composer myself and I must cultivate my own garden.

STEREOPHONY

R.C. What does stereophony mean to you, both as composer and performer, and would you comment on the use of it in present recording technique?

Some Musical Questions

I.S. Our two ears are about six inches apart, whereas the stereo microphones which hear a live orchestra for us are sometimes as much apart as sixty feet. We do not hear live performances stereophonically, therefore, and stereo—instead of giving us 'the best seat in the house'—is, in fact, a kind of non-existent, omnipresent seat. (Nor is it a seat in the orchestra, for an orchestra doesn't sound stereophonic to itself.) I say this not to criticize stereo, however, but to question the meaning of 'high fidelity'. Fidelity to what? But though stereo may be unreal in my sense, it can be in another sense ideal, and as such it has important consequences. For one thing, it is a challenge to existing concert halls; how can we continue to prefer an inferior reality (the concert hall) to ideal stereophony?

The stereo principle that the *distance* between the speakers is the 'microphone', instead of the microphone itself, is still too imperfectly demonstrated by most recordings I have heard, where I have been more conscious of the switch from one speaker to another than of the space between. This ping-pong effect, in certain kinds of music—Wagner's, for example —can be a disturbing distortion, indeed. Wagner's musical-acoustical idea in Bayreuth was to fuse the orchestra, to bring it as close together as possible. Stereophonic separation, with its illusion of orchestral space, is therefore quite alien to his musical intentions. But any purely harmonic music— music that depends on fusion and balance—will suffer from too much focus on its individual parts. In principle, of course, stereophonic recording should be able to fuse and balance, but in practice we often feel as though we are being made to follow the equivalent of an 'Arrow' score,[1] that is, to jump to the violins on their entrance, or swerve in an acoustical spotlight towards the trombones on theirs.

[1] An American edition of orchestral scores in which arrows are used to guide the reader to what is purported to be the leading part.

Some Musical Questions

On the other hand, distortion of this sort does not ruin certain kinds of polyphonic music, for the very reason that this music is poly-phonic, i.e., can be heard from different aural perspectives. Some polyphonic music does not depend on round harmonic balances, and we are even grateful when bits of interior construction are suddenly exposed, or when details of part-writing are brought into relief.

Stereophony also enables us to hear the true effect of many kinds of 'real' stereophonic music, Mozart's *Notturno* for four orchestras, for example, or the *cori spezzati* of the Venetians, music in which the stereophony has been composed rather than engineered. I would also include in this category most of Webern, for a work like his orchestral *Variations*, op. 30, seems to me to exploit the 'distance factor' and to anticipate the new stereophonic idea.

Stereophony has already influenced composed music, too. At one level this amounts to the exploitation of the stereo effect (the stereo fault, rather) by 'building' it 'in', i.e., creating distance and separation by re-seating the orchestra, etc. (When I listen to this sort of music, I find myself *looking* in the direction of the sound, as I do in Cinerama; 'direction' therefore seems to me as good a word as 'distance' to describe the stereo effect.) Stockhausen's *Gruppen* and Boulez's *Doubles* are examples of this influence. At another level, composers will soon come to see that stereo obliges them to construct a more interesting 'middle dimension' in their music.

I cannot contribute very much on the subject of present stereophonic recording techniques, but I do know something about the difficulties conductors experience in satisfying the demands of stereo microphones during recording sessions. Stereophonic separation used to require a separation of orchestral and choral performers, and the various groups of separated instrumentalists and singers are sometimes greatly

125

handicapped in hearing each other; also, solo singers or groups of singers, or perhaps an especially resonant drum, must sometimes be isolated by panels, which makes ensemble playing almost impossible.

In spite of all my reservations about stereo, however, I know that when I am accustomed to it—to its much greater volume and dynamic range, to its really remarkable ability to clarify orchestral doublings (which were probably better left in the dark), to its ability to create the distance between a close instrument and a far-away instrument—I shall be unable to listen to anything else.

TRADITION

Thou bearest not the root, but the root thee.

St. Paul

R.C. Do you have a special theory of, or meaning for, tradition?

I.S. No, I am merely very prudent with the word, for it now seems to imply 'that which resembles the past'—the reason, incidentally, why no good artist is very happy when his work is described as 'traditional'. In fact, the true tradition-making work may not resemble the past at all, and especially not the immediate past, which is the only one most people are able to hear. Tradition is generic; it is not simply 'handed down', fathers to sons, but undergoes a life process: it is born, grows, matures, declines, and is reborn, perhaps. These stages of growth and regrowth are always in contradiction to the stages of another concept or interpretation: true tradition lives in the contradiction. 'Notre héritage n'est précédé d'aucun testament' (Our heritage was left to us by no will).[1]

This is, I think, 'true'. At the same time, however, the artist feels his 'heritage' as the grip of a very strong pair of pincers.

[1] René Char.

THREE OPERAS

1

THE NIGHTINGALE

ITS PREMIÈRE

R.C. Your *Autobiography* contains very little information about the *première* of the Nightingale, nor do other sources describe the event more fully—which is curious if only because the *Nightingale* followed the so sensational *Sacre du Printemps*. What do you remember of the performance and its reception, and why was the production so quickly eclipsed?

I.S. To answer the second question first, the *Nightingale* was introduced only a few weeks before the 1914 war, and during the war the Diaghilev company was too reduced in means to mount anything as complicated as an opera that for only forty-five minutes' playing time required three sets and many costly costumes. The eclipse, as you call it, must be attributed to budgetary rather than artistic reasons.[1] The present neglect of the *Nightingale* is in part due to the fact that it must be performed in a double bill, and suitable companion pieces

[1] Since these remarks were made I have conducted the *Nightingale* in Los Angeles. I now find that Act I, in spite of its very evident Debussyisms, *vocalises a la Lakmé*, and Tchaikovsky melodies too sweet and too cute even for that date, is at least operatic, whereas the later acts are a kind of opera-pageant ballet. I can only attribute the musical style of the later acts—the augmented seconds, parallel intervals, pentatonic tunes, orchestral devices (tremolos, muted brass, cadenzas, etc.) to the great difficulty I experienced in returning to the opera at all after five years, and especially after *Le Sacre du Printemps*.

have been difficult to find (when I conducted it myself at La Scala in the 1920s—a performance efficiently prepared by Toscanini, incidentally—the other half of the bill was . . . *Hansel and Gretel*!). Diaghilev programmed it with ballets, however; and with *Petroushka*, especially, it went very well. Diaghilev always wanted to stage opera as he had staged the *Nightingale*—that is, as opera-ballet, with dancers miming the sung roles, while the singers themselves were nicely out of sight in the orchestra pit.

The *première* was unsuccessful only in the sense that it failed to create a scandal. Musically and visually, the performance was excellent. Monteux conducted capably; the singers—particularly 'Death' and the 'Nightingale'— were good; and, scenically, thanks to Alexander Benois who designed the costumes and sets, it was the most beautiful of all my early Diaghilev works. Boris Romanov composed the dances, and Alexander Sanin was the *metteur en scène*. The opera was sung in Russian; and that is all I remember about the *première*.

        *   *   *

As to its reception, the 'advanced' musicians were genuinely enthusiastic—or so I thought. That Ravel liked it, I am certain, but I am almost as convinced that Debussy did not, for I heard nothing whatever from him about it. I remember this well, for I expected him to question me about the great difference between the music of Act I and the later acts, and though I knew he would have liked the Mussorgsky-Debussy beginning, he probably would have said about that, too, 'Young man, I do it better.' On my last trip to Russia I remember reading a remark in my diary—I kept a diary from 1906 to 1910[1]—written when I was composing the first act of

[1] Left in a steel safe which was part of my grandfather's Biedermeier desk, a piece of furniture which might still be in our house in Oustiloug—together with my manuscripts and letters. Incidentally, all my music before *Petroushka* was written at this desk.

the *Nightingale*: 'Why should I be following Debussy so closely, when the real originator of this operatic style was Mussorgsky?' But, in justice to Debussy, I must own that I saw him only very infrequently in the weeks after the *Nightingale*, and perhaps he simply had no opportunity to tell me his true impressions.

The *Nightingale* was staged in a great hurry. In fact, I was still composing the music only a few months before the *première*. The London performances were probably better than the Parisian, because the singers and dancers would have had more time with their parts. I immensely enjoyed them, at any rate, thanks also to the generosity of Sir Thomas Beecham.[1] I should record the fact, too, that at the outbreak of war Beecham helped me with a payment of money which enabled my mother to return to Russia from Switzerland (by boat from Brindisi to Odessa).

But, rather than attempt to describe the staging of the original *Nightingale*, I will publish Alexander Benois's letters to me covering that period. Benois was in Russia and I in Switzerland during the latter stages of the opera's planning and composition. My wife was ill with tuberculosis and we moved to Leysin—to be near the sanatorium. I could not meet Benois, therefore, which was a misfortune, though it produced these letters. Benois was the conservative of the company, and Diaghilev tended to favour Roerich, not Benois, as the *Nightingale*'s designer. I had great respect for Benois, however, and insisted that he decorate my opera. Benois's ideas *were* followed, and his suggestions in the fourth letter are, in fact, an exact 'in colour' account of the actual staging.

[1] I think it was on this trip, though it may have been the year before, that I met Frederick Delius. He had come to Covent Garden to attend a performance of our Ballet. Beecham introduced him to me, and he paid me compliments for *Petroushka*, but, as I spoke almost no English, and he but little French, the conversation did not develop. Thirty-seven years later, I visited his famous orange farm, D. H. Lawrence's would-have-been Utopia, in Florida.

Three Operas

1

Dear Igor Feodorovitch,

My dear friend, how sad that we are living so far apart. It seems to me that we could do great things together! But this way nothing will happen. And all the others are dispersed, too. Serge is the Devil knows where. After discussing the Bach ballet with me in Baden, he was to have come to see me in Lugano and to have brought Ravel with him. But I have heard nothing from him, and since he has disappeared without a note, I am inclined to believe those charming gossipers (their news has probably reached you too) who say that Vaslav married a Hungarian millionairess and Serge, in his grief, has sold the company to an impresario. Have you any news of our dissolute genius Serge? Valetchka,[1] who went to Paris (cursing his fate, poor fellow), also does not know anything.

Besides the staging of the Goldoni I must also start to prepare *The Possessed* for the spring season, and all this in addition to writing my *History of Painting*. I am passionately interested in the *Nightingale*. When do you think it will be ready for its run? I do not give up hope of doing it myself. It would be a creative aphrodisiac for me. I believe that Roerich would achieve something miraculous with it, but some details Roerich would probably not do, and just these details would interest me enormously.

My dear friend, write to me again, and soon. I promise to answer without delay, and if you want some information I will be glad to help you. I embrace you and I kiss the hand of dear Catherina Gabrielovna, to whom my wife sends her most cordial greetings.

Your loving,
ALEXANDER BENOIS

[1] Walter Nouvel.

2

St. Petersburg,
28th September 1913

Dear Igor Feodorovitch, I was in Moscow and found your letter only on my return. The news about Nijinsky's marriage struck me like a thunderbolt. When did it happen? None of our friends is here in town at the moment, and I know of no one who can give me any information about it, since I do not want to talk to a stranger like Svetlov.[1] I saw Serge and Vaslav almost on the eve of Vaslav's departure for Argentina, and there was no hint then about the coming event. Nijinsky was very attentively studying Bach with us, preparing the Bach ballet. Is it possible that he had no idea of it then? Be kind and tell me one thing: was it a complete surprise for Serge, or was he prepared for it? How deep was his shock?[2] Their romance was coming to an end, and I doubt that he was really heartbroken, but if he did suffer I hope it was not too terrible for him. However, I imagine he must be completely bewildered in his position as head of the company. But why can't Nijinsky be both a ballet master and a Hungarian millionaire?[3] The whole story is such a phantasmagoria I sometimes think I have read it in a dream and am an idiot to believe it.

I am sorry to be unable to fulfil your request completely, but listen why: the two theatres have become rivals, and all connections between them are broken. The gossip I hear about it has been contradictory and I do not know what to believe. Some people say everything in the Free Theatre is perfect: that there is plenty of money; that each invention is more amusing and ingenious than the one before; that two

[1] A well-known balletomane.
[2] I had been with Diaghilev in the Montreux Palace Hotel when the news of Nijinsky's marriage came, and I had watched him turn into a madman who begged me and my wife not to leave him alone.
[3] Benois evidently thought Nijinsky had married a Hungarian heiress.

of the subscription nights are already sold out (this, it seems, is true), etc., etc. . . .

Some people are delighted by Mardzhanov, but others say he is impossible, etc., etc. I personally think that, in any case, it will last at least two years and that they will be able to stage the *Nightingale*,[1] but I would not promise it absolutely. I think also that they will do a mixture, some interesting things and much *merde*. The Moscow public will swallow it all, good and bad alike, of course, since Moscow knows no better and will devour anything. I am very impatient for the opening, however, because a venture as naïve as *that* must at least result in something refreshing.

I am longing for the *Nightingale*, especially after seeing Mitusov, who gave me his impressions after Warsaw.[2]

I embrace you. As soon as I have something more definite I will write you. I kiss Catherina Gabrielovna's hand and send you best wishes. With love,

ALEXANDER BENOIS

3

St. Petersburg,
1st January 1914

Dear Igor Feodorovitch, I write in a hurry as I am just leaving for Moscow. For the last two hours I have looked everywhere for your letter with the description of the sets (and the enumeration of the characters), and cannot find it. I could start to study the play and just now comes this delay. I beg you, send me immediately a second copy, and also a detailed libretto. I beg you not to insist on the colours. I have my own ideas, and I think the result will be good. The hall in the castle will be pink with dark blue and black. But, my God,

---

[1] The *Nightingale* was produced at the Imperial Theatre in 'Petrograd', January, 1916, staged by Meyerhold and decorated by Golovine.

[2] I had been with Mitusov in Warsaw to discuss the *Nightingale* libretto. I was on my way from Russia to Switzerland, where I finished the composition of the opera.

where is the music? Is it possible that I will have to work without this main source of inspiration and without your personal promptings?

Goodness, the train!!! I embrace you cordially,

Your,

ALEXANDER BENOIS

P.S. Write to me c/o Moscow Art Theatre, Kammergersky Drive. *Come!*

4

Moscow,
15th February 1914

Dear Igor Feodorovitch, Although your so obstinate silence shows that you do not wish to talk to me at all, I am obliged to bother you to clarify a few points. (I flatter myself, however, and hope that the real reason for your silence is not a change of your feelings towards me, but circumstances which have enveloped you as much as they have me.)

The hall of the Emperor will be white with blue.[1] On the other hand there will be a lot of pink and green in the costumes. But what keeps me from finishing the sketch of this setting and of the set in this tableau in general, is this: what am I to do with the procession? You wanted a palanquin and you wanted the Emperor 'inserted' in the throne.[2] A marvellous idea! But how do you visualize the following combination: the throne is carried by a whole crowd of people, including eight small children; the throne is put on a scaffold, and then the Emperor appears, surrounded closely by dignitaries who hold five parasols above *Him*! You wanted a palanquin, but every procession has one, and *this* is new.

In general, I am constructing the procession as follows:

---

[1] Sic. See letter 3.
[2] My idea was to have the Emperor fixed on his throne like a doll. (I.S.)

137

seven female dancers dressed in gold;

seven female dancers dressed in silver;

one male dancer and one female dancer very luxuriously costumed, and with them three dancers; monsters, and two white boys with swords, and five black boys with swords; all this party participating in a symbolic pantomime.

After this comes the court (the chorus is already on the stage):

first appear two white-costumed mandarins;

then—two grey-costumed mandarins;

then—a totally black Grand Master of the Court;

then—the Chief Chamberlain with the Nightingale.

Then comes the throne, and finally, His Majesty, whom nobody could see until this moment because of the parasols hiding him.

The procession closes with two soldiers who take a standing position at the foot of the throne. (The same kind of soldiers can walk in front, or be ready on the stage in the beginning.)

Do you see now what I mean? But perhaps you want something quite different. The final word is with you, but for God's sake, send me this word immediately, or everything will go to hell. Until I have your exact instructions I shall not start the definitive work.

Perhaps an even more important question concerns the last act. How do you see it yourself? And, first of all, I beg you to send me the details of the staging immediately, and the libretto itself, which I ask you to mark with the basic tempi. This is supremely important (the music will explain what I shall not understand in the text). I would prefer to have the piano score, but probably it is far from finished.

How can we see each other to discuss all this? I wanted to come to Berlin for a meeting but now it is simply impossible. Think only how many days will be wasted, and just now, when every hour is precious. Is it absolutely impossible for you to come here?

Now, about the *décor* of the third act. I imagine it like this: in front is a kind of antechamber, separated from the bedroom by a big curtain (covering the whole stage: red, yellow, gold, and black). This curtain is first drawn back and we see a majestic bedroom at night and in moonlight. The curtains are then closed and at the end again opened for us to see a Sacrum Cubiculum in all its splendour (many windows, a gigantic bed, etc.). What do you think of it? Perhaps you have conceived it quite differently? I implore you to answer.

I kiss Catherina Gabrielovna's hand and wish with all my heart happiness for the newborn baby,[1] the mother and the happy father. I am burning with impatience to embrace you. One of these days I expect to hear Kussevitsky conduct *Le Sacre du Printemps*. I embrace you,

ALEXANDER BENOIS

P.S. Write me to St. Petersburg, 31, Admirals' Canal, and on the envelope write 'in case of absence please forward the letter immediately'. But the best thing to do, my dear, would be to answer the main points by telegram. If you are in agreement with all: 'Approuve tout'; if not, then in a few words: 'Emperor en palanquin'; 'Trône en scène', etc. Something of this kind. For God's sake, hurry with an answer.

5

St. Petersburg,
14th–17th February 1914

Dear Igor Feodorovitch, I am in a great rush, for which reason I will limit myself to business and avoid speaking about my artistic feelings.

It is already a whole week that I have been living with the

---

[1] My daughter, Maria Milena.

sounds of *Le Sacre du Printemps* in my ears. It started in
Moscow and continues now in St. Petersburg. I am longing
to hear it again, and am sad when I think that for a long
time I shall be unable to hear this music, about which I cannot even say if it is good or great, because I am still completely bewildered by it. Nor do I know if Kussevitsky conducted it correctly. However, we have our impressions of it.

The success, alas, was rather big, in spite of the hundred
people who walked out after the first part. I say 'alas' because
the audience applauded in advance, in defiance of Paris, and
also because *that* audience applauds Bach, Beethoven,
Wagner, Rachmaninov, and Stravinsky all equally. (Do not
carry your head too high, and do not draw conclusions, but I
love the first of these names and very much dislike most of
the others.) A success with such an audience is nauseating. I
am very glad that Nurok liked it, however; and that the
Rimsky-Korsakov clan hissed it violently is also a consolation.

I babble too much. Business! Business! My dear, what
about the following combination: in the beginning, a huge
bedroom with a few windows flooded by moonlight; ghosts
(Serge does not want ghosts but why not have them sitting on
the bed or showing their ugly faces through the curtain of the
bed—I do not yet know myself exactly how to do it); a bed
with a canopy; a catafalque through which 'Death' leaves
(not through the window; the catafalque must melt in front
of you—is such a trick possible?). Day breaks during the
Nightingale's song. Then, with the bird's last notes, the courtiers, thinking the Emperor dead, ceremoniously close the
curtains (the courtiers walk on stage, single file).

The next scene, the court, is in front of the stage curtain,
so that when the curtain goes up the bedroom can be flooded
by sunlight for the Emperor's 'Bonjour à tous'. Apropos this
finale, I thought the ending of the *Sacre* perhaps too abrupt

—lacking in the feeling of finality. People who saw the stage performance say that it is even more noticeable there. I am afraid such a thing can happen again; but, of course, you must know better. Do not listen to that monster Serge, who has a mania to cut and will cut until nothing is left. I await your confirmation of the plans, or any changes that have to be made.

The set for the second tableau is already done, and whether it is good or bad I cannot say because I have no time to look at it again.

Anna Karlovna[1] had a sore throat and could not be present at the *Sacre*. She sends you and dear Catherina Gabrielovna, whom we both love with all our hearts, our greetings and best wishes.

Devotedly yours,

ALEXANDER BENOIS

P.S. My family all praise the *Nightingale* sets, but how can one believe one's family?

P.P.S. I know nothing about the Free Theatre beyond what has been written in the newspapers. I hear, however, that Mardzhanov found another idiot willing to give money and that he wants to ruin this new idiot by introducing spectacles of dramatic action.

Sanin will stay with Suhodolsky and will stage operettas, probably. Since I came back from Moscow, where I did the *décors* and sets for Goldoni's *Tavern Keeper*, I am so deep in the *Nightingale*, I have no time to read or to learn anything. I see no one, and I have had no conversation with anybody.

I embrace you devotedly, dear Igor Feodorovitch, and again wish you everything that is good. And, once more, please give my greetings to your charming wife,

---

[1] Mme Benois,

Three Operas

6

St. Jean de Luz,
Hotel de la Porte,
23rd July 1914

My dear friend, your letter puzzled me so much I have gone around composing answers to it for the last five days, but I cannot manage a single one. I really do not like Kozma Prootkov,[1] or rather, I do not understand the gigantic importance he assumes in Russian literature and in Russian life. Kozma Prootkov is funny, foolish, clever, and from time to time extremely talented, but the book never shows a really strong sense of humour, or the real art of laughter of Gogol and Dostoievsky. At any rate, I do not see real wit in Prootkov's too long and naïve—in the bad sense—salad of parody. So, in my opinion, it is not worthwhile spending time on Prootkov, and I think it would be better to forget this 'manual for Russian schoolboys', this copybook for our *Satirikon* and *Boodilnik*.[2] Laughter must be different now, funnier and more terrible. Nevertheless, I read the book from the first page to the last (by the way, I thank you for it, because it gave me great pleasure, nevertheless). Your rapture over it perplexed me and I wished with all my heart to feel the same. Alas, this did not happen, and I was left a cold fish. I decided to be frank and to tell you the truth, but my truth is not absolute, and I would be unhappy indeed if my opinion were to disconcert you. Perhaps you find something where I see only emptiness. If so, start work. Though I hold to my opinion, I am sure that Kozma Prootkov as seen by Stravinsky will start to live a new and wonderful life. Also, I am sure that

---

[1] Under this imaginary name, three well-known Russian poets of the 1860s, Alexei Tolstoy and the brothers Jemchooshnikov, wrote a book of humorous and nonsensical verse that was very popular in Tsarist Russia. I had proposed a collaboration with Benois to make a comic piece for the theatre, a kind of *Renard*, to some verses and a little play from Kozma Prootkov.

[2] Russian humorous magazines.

listening to your music (and I believe in every note) I shall be able to catch your feelings and create something worthy of your music—or, at least, something that will not spoil it. But perhaps you should choose another painter, for instance, Sudeikine, who is under-rated and who, more swiftly than I, will find response in his soul to what Jemchooshnikov and Tolstoy fabricated.

My dear, I am very worried about the impression this 'cold-water' letter will make on you and your muse, but cold water is not so bad if it comes at the proper time and if you have a towel handy. If my douche was mistimed and you catch cold, please forgive me, dear.

With love and kisses for you both,

ALEXANDER BENOIS

2

PERSEPHONE

R.C. Your autobiography did not reveal the circumstances of your collaboration with André Gide. To what extent was *Persephone* in fact a collaboration? And, as Gide was one of your first acquaintances in Paris, would you describe him as you knew him?

I.S. Gide is a complicated subject in any case, and he was not less so personally. He had to be prised open, like an oyster, and the priser had to remember not to put his fingers in the wrong place, for, like an oyster, he could bite. If I were to hear someone else describe him I think I could comment on the accuracy of the description, but for me to talk about such a man myself is difficult indeed.

We met for the first time in 1910, in Misia Sert's rooms at the Hotel Meurice. I knew him by reputation, of course: he was already an established writer, though his fame was to come much later. After that I saw him from time to time at ballet rehearsals. Whether he came to those of *Le Sacre du Printemps*, however, I do not know. (But I was too busy with *Le Sacre* to be aware of anyone besides Debussy and Ravel, who were not then on speaking terms and who sat on opposite sides of the house; I took my place directly behind Mon-

21. With Gide in Wiesbaden, 1933

22. With Charles Chaplin, Hollywood, 1937
Photograph by King Vidor, courtesy of *Life Magazine*

Three Operas

teux to avoid a show of partiality for either of the feuding composers. Debussy, incidentally, was very amiable about *Le Sacre* at the rehearsals, which made his later, negative attitude all the more surprising.)

Some months after *Le Sacre* Gide approached me with a project to compose incidental music for his translation of *Antony and Cleopatra*. I replied that the musical style would depend on the style of the whole production, but he did not understand what I meant. Later, when I suggested that the production be in modern dress, he was shocked—and deaf to my arguments that we would be nearer Shakespeare by inventing something new, and nearer him in every way than he was, veristically, to Antony and Cleopatra. I still believe, by the way, that the music in Shakespeare's plays should be Shakespearean, i.e., period music, and that even Purcell's Shakespearean pieces should be performed only with a style of production appropriate to the period; and, of course, 'modern' music is justified only in 'modern' versions of the plays. (Sound effects—electronic music—are something apart; I am talking about musical style.)

As for *Persephone*, I hardly think it can be called a collaboration. The only parts of the libretto we had actually worked on together were the children's choruses; I wished to repeat the music here and asked Gide to compose additional verses (as, later, I was to ask Auden for a second set of choruses in Act I, scene 2, of the *Rake*).

His *Persephone* was an early work and quite unknown to me. Madame Ida Rubinstein had asked me to read it and to meet Gide to discuss the possibility of a collaboration based upon it. A dance-mime role would have to be created for her, of course, but we understood that to be the only stipulation. (Mme Rubinstein was an actress and a woman of great wealth. I had known her since my arrival in Paris in 1910, and I attended the first performance of Debussy's *Le Martyre*

K

de Saint Sébastien with her and d'Annunzio, in her box. She was also an 'original', as she proved in her eighteenth year by hiring a private train to take her from St. Petersburg to Moscow. She had commissioned Bakst to arrange the flower beds of her Paris garden so that all the flowers were in trays and the whole garden could be changed every few weeks. I often saw Gide at her Paris home.) Gide came to Wiesbaden to see me in 1933. We read his original *Persephone* together and decided at once on the device of the speaker and on the three-part form. Gide reconstructed and rewrote the original book after this meeting.

These are some of the letters I received from Gide during our 'collaboration':

1

1 bis rue Vaneau,
Paris VII,
20th January 1933

My dear friend, Ida Rubinstein has asked me to write to you. She has been seduced by an idea, which I have just submitted to her, for a symphonic ballet. She says that if it seduces you also, you will agree to work with me for her. The thought of attaching my name to your name in a work that has been close to my heart for a very long time fills me with extreme pride and joy. A word from you would call me to Berlin or elsewhere to talk to you about it—and the sooner the better. I will dine Monday the 23rd at Ida's with Sert, who is very enthusiastic and who would like to do the settings. I could join you Wednesday. It does not matter where.

A word from you or a telegram to Ida Rubinstein or to me would tell us where to telephone you Monday evening between nine and ten o'clock (don't forget the difference in time, and what is the number?).

This moment Ida Rubinstein telephones me to say that you expect to reach the south of France soon where I could then join you. And perhaps you will come through Paris, which would save my coming to Berlin.

Amicalement, and full of hope,

ANDRÉ GIDE

2

8th February 1933

My dear friend,

First of all, let me tell you of the excellent impressions I have brought back with me from our meeting in Wiesbaden. I told Mme. Rubinstein that our understanding was perfect. Without exaggeration, I am sure that we will find in her our best support in the struggle with even the most exacting designer, whoever he may be. She is extremely pleased with what I told her about the way in which you understood the subject as the celebration of a mystery, and that you want to remove from the libretto what I was at first tempted to put in: episodic bits—as though for a kind of *divertissement*. I am now working in this direction.

I will send you an edition of the Odyssey (in translation) that contains the Homeric hymns. It is the last of these hymns (to Demeter) which inspired me, and I do not doubt that you will find in it the same extraordinary exaltation which I found myself when I read it the first time. All my efforts will be towards maintaining the nobility of this exaltation throughout my text.

As you will feel for yourself, the subject itself is halfway between a natural interpretation (the rhythm of the seasons; the corn falling in the soil must die to be resurrected through the sleep of winter) and a mystical interpretation; this way the myth is connected at the same time with both the ancient Egyptian cults and Christian doctrine.

147

Three Operas

I was much moved by what you said to me in Wiesbaden: that it will be interesting to mark and to fix the change of seasons, and the feeling of the seasonal cycle is indispensable to our melodrama. But this idea of starting with the Autumn (however seductive it may be as an idea for beginning the descent of Proserpina into Hell) cannot be maintained. It would be cheating the Greek myth too outrageously, and you will see why when you read the Hymn to Demeter. Proserpina has nothing to do with Autumn. (Besides, the Greek year had only three seasons.) She is the purest personification of the *Spring*.

The plan of the first scene will follow in two days. It consists of recitation, dances, and songs. Mme Rubinstein says it is impossible for the chorus to dance or for the dancing nymphs to sing. Therefore, it will probably be necessary to place the chorus in the orchestra pit or to one side of the stage front: this will have to be studied. What is most important to me is to know, after my plan, how much time this first scene will take.

Very attentively and cordially yours,
ANDRÉ GIDE

Grand Hotel,
Le Lavandou,
Var,
24th February 1933

My dear Igor, This short note to welcome your return to Voreppe which you said would be on the 25th. I am working 'like a dog' for you. By now you should have received the sketch of the first scene. I consider the text as definitive only in so far as it suits you. The same with the second scene, which I gave to be typed today and which you will receive very soon (in one or two days).

The part of the speaker (Eumolpus, the founder and first

officiating priest of the Eleusinian mysteries) should be played by a baritone, the part of Pluto by a bass, the bass-est bass possible, and the chorus by women's voices only. As you will see, I decided, at your invitation, to exclude everything anecdotal. Even the character of Eurydice. I fear that this scene (the meeting with Eurydice), completely episodic as it is, will make it too long. I could add this scene, however, if the text seems to you too short for the musical development, as it now seems to me.

Madame Rubinstein seems to be very pleased. I want you to be pleased, too, and I will listen with attention to all your criticisms, remarks, suggestions, etc.

Wishing you fruitful work, I am, full of hope and expectations,

Very affectionately yours,

ANDRÉ GIDE

4

1 bis rue Vaneau,
Paris VII,
8th August 1933

My dear Igor, Excuse this delay. I found your letter yesterday evening coming back from a small trip in Belgium.

Encore is written (in poetry) either with or without the final *e*, depending on the requirements of the rhythm and the rhyme. I propose—*ad libitum*—for the second verse: *Parle encor Parle encor, princesse Perséphone*, which is better than my previous proposal.

Parle-nous, parle-nous encor Perséphone

is perfectly possible without *e* (and so would satisfy your wish for two syllables) but the verse would have only eleven feet because we do not count the final syllable as a foot if it is a silent 'e'.

It seems to me that according to the musical indication you

gave me *Parle encor Parle encor, princesse Perséphone* would work perfectly.

Happy to know you are working well. I shake your hand.

Amicalement,

ANDRÉ GIDE

*　　　　　*　　　　　*

There are at least two explanations for Gide's dislike of my *Persephone* music. One is that the musical accentuation of the text surprised and displeased him, though he had been warned in advance that I would stretch and stress and otherwise 'treat'[1] French as I had Russian, and though he understood my ideal texts to be syllable poems, the haiku of Bashō and Buson, for example, in which the words do not impose strong tonic accentuation of their own.[2] The other explanation is simply that he could not follow my musical speech. When I first played the music to him at Ida Rubinstein's he would only say 'c'est curieux, c'est très curieux', and disappeared as soon afterwards as possible. He did not attend the rehearsals, and if he was present at any of the performances *I* did not see him. A play of his was then being staged in the Petit Théâtre des Champs-Elysées, but this shouldn't have prevented him from hearing at least one performance of *Persephone*. Shortly after the *première* he sent me a copy of the newly published libretto with the dedication 'in communion'. I answered that 'communion' was exactly what we had not had; his last letter to me is in reply to that.

[1] I will admit, however, that my habits of musical accentuation have misled meaning in at least one instance. The line *Ego senem cecidi* in *Oedipus Rex* accented on the *ce*, as I have it, means 'I fell the old man', whereas it should be accented *Ego senem cecídi* and mean 'I killed the old man'. This can be corrected in performance, but remains awkward.

[2] Since making these remarks I have witnessed an instance of word treatment similar to my own in the Kanjinchō play (Kabuki Theatre). Here, in the famous catechism scene between Togashi and Benkei, a verse dialogue I did not have to understand to enjoy as music, the verbs are syncopated, I am told, held over the bar lines, so to speak, and the syllables grouped into rhythmic quantities that tend to obscure sense.

Three Operas

1 bis rue Vaneau,
28th May 1934

My dear Stravinsky,

I hope, none the less, you will not put in doubt my affection for you and my admiration for your work, because I did not attend the rehearsals of your, of our, *Persephone*! Or do you harbour some other grievance against me that I do not know of?

As I have no grievance of any kind against you, I will continue in my ardent friendship for you.

ANDRÉ GIDE

We did not meet again after *Persephone*, but I do not think we were really angry with each other even then. Indeed, how could anyone be angry for long with a man of so much honesty?

*   *   *

If I could distinguish between Gide's talent and his writing, it would be to proclaim a preference for the latter, though the writing, too, is very often like *eau distillée*. I considered the *Voyage au Congo* the best of his books, but I did not care for either the spirit or the approach in his fiction: he was not grand enough as a creator to make us forget the sins of his nature—as Tolstoy can make us forget the sins of *his* nature. However, as he seldom talked about his work my relations with him were smooth in this respect.

Though Gide was not a conspicuously loving critic he was at least inside the art he criticized. And his criticism could and did illuminate. His limitation, I thought, was his 'reason': all he did or said had to be reasoned, with the result that he lacked enthusiasm and could find no sympathy for all the vast unreasonableness in man and art. 'It is better to reason,' he would say, 'than to make an enthusiastic mistake.' That he had wit is evident from his reply when asked to name the greatest French poet: 'Hélas, Victor Hugo.' And verbal precision such as he had is always enviable; I would have esteemed him if only for that. But he was at his best in company, with Valéry, or Claudel, or Ramuz, for then the conversation would always revert to the French language, and on this subject he was without peer.

Gide was fascinated by Pushkin, and he would sometimes call on me in my Paris apartment to talk to me about the Russian poet and indeed about everything Russian. He called on me in Berlin, too, in October 1931, an occasion I also remember because of Hindemith's having bravely chastised the Berlin Radio Orchestra for its bad playing of my new violin concerto. Apart from Pushkin and Russia his favourite conversational subject was religion. I had returned to the Orthodox Church in 1926 (I became a Communicant then for the first time since 1910 and composed my first religious work, an a cappella *Pater Noster*[1]) and was not a good quarry for his proselytizing Protestantism, but I have more respect for him and his views than for some of the Catholic Pharisees who ridiculed him.

*　　　　*　　　　*

I do not know how to describe him in appearance. He was quite undistinguished and he must have wished to become even more so by dressing like a *petit bourgeois*. And the one physical characteristic of his I can remember is also negative. When he spoke, only his lips and mouth moved: his body and

---

[1] I composed the *Pater Noster* and, later, an *Ave Maria* and a *Credo*, for use in the Russian Orthodox Church. In accordance with liturgical tradition, and in view of the Eastern Church fiat prohibiting the use of musical instruments (even of pitch pipes), the music is a simple harmonic intonation of the words. I heard the *Pater Noster* for the first time in the Russian Church in the rue Daru, Paris, by surprise, at the funeral of a Beliankin cousin. In 1949 I prepared a Latin version of all three pieces, revising the *Ave Maria* somewhat in the process.

the rest of his face remained perfectly immobile and expres-
sionless. He also smiled a little smile which I thought ironic
and which may or may not have been—though I thought it
was—a sign of inner torment. But if I had not known so much
about Gide wouldn't I have been more open with him myself?

3

THE RAKE'S PROGRESS

R.C. How did you come to choose the 'Rake's Progress' as the subject, and W. H. Auden as the librettist, of your opera? How much of the plot and how many of the characters, the scenes, and the sequences of musical numbers were conceived and planned by you together with Auden? What are your present thoughts about the style and construction of the opera?

I.S. Hogarth's 'Rake's Progress' paintings, which I saw in 1947 on a chance visit to the Chicago Art Institute, immediately suggested a series of operatic scenes to me. I was, however, readily susceptible to such a suggestion for I had wanted to compose an opera in English ever since my arrival in the United States. I chose Auden on the recommendation of my good friend and neighbour Aldous Huxley: at that time all I knew of his work was the commentary for the film *Night Train*. When I had described to Huxley the kind of verse opera I wished to write he assured me Auden was the poet with whom I could write it. Accordingly, in October 1947, I wrote to Auden telling him of my 'Rake's Progress' idea. He replied as follows:

Three Operas

7 Cornelia Street,
New York 14, N.Y.,
12th October 1947

Dear Mr. Stravinsky,

Thank you very much for your letter of October 6th, which arrived this morning.

As you say, it is a terrible nuisance being thousands of miles apart, but we must do the best we can.

As (*a*) you have thought about the Rake's Progress for some time, and (*b*) it is the librettist's job to satisfy the composer, not the other way round, I should be most grateful if you could let me have any ideas you may have formed about characters, plot, etc.

I think the Asylum finale sounds excellent, but, for instance, if he is to play the fiddle then, do you want the fiddle to run through the story?

You speak of a 'free verse preliminary'. Do you want the arias and ensembles to be finally written in free verse or only as a basis for discussing the actual form they should take? If they were spoken, the eighteenth-century style would of course demand rhyme but I know how different this is when the words are set.

I have an idea, which may be ridiculous, that between the two acts, there should be a choric parabasis as in Aristophanes.

I need hardly say that the chance of working with you is the greatest honour of my life.

Yours very sincerely,

WYSTAN AUDEN

P.S. I hope you can read my writing. Unfortunately, I do not know how to type.

I then invited him to come to my house in California where

we could work together. On 24th October I received the following telegram from him:

MANY THANKS FOR WIRE AND GENEROUS OFFER SHAME-
FACEDLY ACCEPTED SUGGEST LEAVING NEW YORK
NOVEMBER TENTH IF CONVENIENT FOR YOU.   WYSTAN
AUDEN.

He arrived at night carrying a small bag and a huge cow-
skin rug, a gift for me from an Argentine friend. My wife had
been anxious that our only extra bed, a studio couch, might
not be long enough for him, but when we saw this big, blond,
intellectual bloodhound on our front porch (before an hour
had elapsed, however, we knew he was going to be a very
gentle and lovable bloodhound, however super-intellectual)
we realized that we hadn't been anxious enough. He slept
with his body on the couch and his feet, covered by a blanket
pinioned with books, on a nearby chair, like the victim of a
more humane and reasonable Procrustes.

Early the next morning, primed by coffee and whisky, we
began work on the *Rake's Progress*. Starting with a hero, a
heroine, and a villain, and deciding that these people should
be a tenor, a soprano, and a bass, we proceeded to invent a
series of scenes leading up to the final scene in Bedlam that
was already fixed in our minds. We followed Hogarth closely
at first and until our own story began to assume a different
significance.

Mother Goose and the Ugly Duchess were Auden's con-
tributions, of course, but the plot and the scheme of action
were worked out by the two of us together, step by step. We
also tried to co-ordinate the plan of action with a provisional
plan of musical pieces, arias, ensembles, and choruses. Auden
kept saying, 'Let's see, now . . . ah, ah, ah . . . let's see . . .
ah , . , ah. . . .', and I the equivalent in Russian, but after ten

days we had completed an outline[1] which is not radically different from the published libretto.

*   *   *

Auden fascinated and delighted me more every day. When we were not working he would explain verse forms to me, and almost as quickly as he could write, compose examples; I still have a specimen sestina and some light verse that he scribbled off for my wife; and any technical question, of versification, for example, put him in a passion; he was even eloquent on such matters.

The making of poetry he seemed to regard as a game, albeit to be played in a magic circle. The latter had already been drawn; Auden's task, as he considered it, was to redefine and be the custodian of its rules. All his conversation about Art was, so to speak, *sub specie ludi.*

I still remember some of the things he said on that first visit—though not, alas, his exact words. He was forever putting forth little Scholastic or psycho-analytic propositions: 'Angels are pure intellect'; 'Tristan and Isolde were unloved only children'; Pelléas had 'alarming trichomaniac tendencies; the sign of a man's loss of power is when he ceases to care about punctuality' (Auden himself lived by the clock—'I am hungry only if the clock says it is time to eat') 'and of the woman's, when she stops caring about dress'. These, too, were—so they seemed—part of the game.

I was puzzled at first by what I took to be contradictions in his personality. He would sail on steady rudders of reason and logic yet profess to curious, if not superstitious, beliefs—in graphology, for instance (I have a graphological chart with an analysis of his writing, the souvenir of an evening in Venice), in astrology, in the telepathic powers of cats, in black magic (as it is described in Charles Williams's

[1] See Appendix, p. 167.

157

novels), in categories of temperament (I was a 'Dionysian' if I happened to work at night), in preordination, in Fate. Another, though more apparent than real, contradiction in him was his display of good citizenship. However lofty his criticism of Society, he was almost too conscientious in fulfilling his everyday democratic duties. He would even serve on juries (I remember his having stalled one for two weeks: 'not for Justice, of course—I quite understood the point involved—but because the housewife jurists were motivated purely by revenge'). He was properly and justly outraged by us for our failure to vote.

Auden's mind was didactic, but it was also, for me anyway, happily heuristic. Few people have taught me as much, and after he left, books he had talked about from Groddeck to de Tocqueville began to appear in our library. Nor do I confine his influence on me to literature, for however good his literary criticism (and why haven't his pieces on Santayana, on Yeats, and on so many others, been collected?), he always seemed to me more profound as a moralist—indeed, he is one of the few moralists whose tone I can bear.

*   *   *

I recall only two events of his visit, apart from our work. One day he complained of pressure in his ears. We took him to a doctor who removed large wax globes from each ear. Auden was intrigued by this and kept referring to the 'extraordinary little creatures' that had been harbouring in his auditory canals. We also attended a two-piano performance of *Così fan tutti* together—an omen, perhaps, for the *Rake* is deeply involved in *Così*.

*   *   *

The following letters came from Auden after his return to New York:

158

Three Operas

7 Cornelia Street,
New York 14, N.Y.,
20th November 1947

Dear Mrs. Stravinsky,

First, an account of my stewardship, I have

(a) Posted the letter to the Guggenheim Foundation.

(b) Called Miss Bean.

(c) Called Mr. Heinsheimer.

The journey was a nightmare. The flight was cancelled; I was transferred to an American Airlines local which left at 7:00 A.M., stopped *everywhere* and reached New York at 4 A.M. this morning. The meals, as usual, would have tried the patience of a stage curate, so you can imagine what I felt, after a week of your luxurious cuisine. And finally, of course, I got back here to a pile of silly letters to answer—a job I loathe. The only consolation is the pleasure of my writing you this bread-and-butter letter (how do you say that in Russian?). I loved every minute of my stay, thanks to you both, and shall look forward with impatience to the next time we meet.

Greetings to Vassily, Das krankheitliebendes Fräulein, Popka, Mme Sokolov, La Baroness des Chats, etc.[1]

Yours ever,
WYSTAN AUDEN

P.S. Could you give the enclosed note to the maestro?

(Enclosed note)—Du Syllabiste—Au compositeur.

---

[1] Vassily was our cat; the 'illness-loving Fräulein' *is* our housekeeper, Evgenia Petrovna; Popka, our parrot—we had forty parrots and lovebirds at that time—was the special favourite of Evgenia Petrovna and a relationship alarmingly like that in Flaubert's *Félicité* existed between them; Mme Sokolov was the wife of the actor and a dear friend and neighbour; the Baroness was Catherine d'Erlanger, another friend and neighbour.

Cher Igor Stravinsky,
 Memo. Act I, Sc. 1,

Je crois que ça sera mieux si c'est un oncle inconnu du héros au lieu de son père qui meurt, parce que comme ça, la richesse est tout à fait imprévue, et la note pastorale n'est pas interrompue par le douteur, seulement par la présence sinistre du villain. En ce cas, la girl possèdera un père, pas un oncle.

Etes-vous d'accord? Je tiendrai silence pour oui,

WYSTAN AUDEN

P.S. I can't tell you what a pleasure it is to collaborate with you. I was so frightened that you might be a *prima donna*.

Salut au 'making'

*   *   *

7 *Cornelia Street*,
New York 14, N.Y.,
16th January 1948

Dear Igor Stravinsky,

Herewith Act I. As you will see, I have taken in a collaborator, an old friend of mine in whose talents I have the greatest confidence.[1]

We are in the middle of Act II now, which I will send as soon as it is done.

I've marked places where cuts in the text can be easily made if you want to, but of course, don't hesitate to make cuts of your own.

With warmest remembrances to Mrs. Stravinsky and everyone else.

Yours ever,
WYSTAN AUDEN

*   *   *

[1] Chester Kallman, who, in fact, wrote the latter part of the first scene (after the aria 'Since it is not by merit'), and the entire second scene; the first scene of Act II to the end of Tom's aria 'Vary the song', and the entire

I was delighted with the first act, but afraid it might be too long.

Auden telegraphed:

24th January 1948

MANY THANKS FOR WIRE WILL MAIL ACT TWO MONDAY DO NOT WORRY ABOUT EXCESSIVE LENGTH WHICH CAN BE CUT AD LIB WHEN WE MEET HOPE YOU COME IN MARCH BEFORE I LEAVE APRIL SEVENTH. WYSTAN AUDEN.

*   *   *

7 Cornelia Street,
New York 14, N.Y.,
28th January 1948

Dear Igor Stravinsky,

Voici Acte II. It seemed best to transfer the Auction Scene to Act III, as that is where the time interval occurs. Have made a few slight alterations in our original plot in order to make each step of the Rake's Progress unique, i.e.:

Bordel   —Le plaisir.
Baba   —L'acte gratuit.
La Machine—Il désire devenir Dieu.

As I said in my wire, don't worry about length. Once you have the whole material to look at, you can form your own opinions and it won't be hard to make cuts and alterations.

Yours ever,
WYSTAN AUDEN

*   *   *

I saw him next in the Hotel Raleigh (in the 'Lily Pons Suite', to be exact), Washington, D. C., on 31st March 1948.

second scene; the first scene of Act III (except for the off-stage lines of Tom and Shadow) and the card-guessing game in scene two. Auden, of course, wrote the rest.

He had shown the finished libretto to T. S. Eliot meanwhile (Eliot had noted one split infinitive and one anachronism— 'alluvial', I think; 'fluminous' would have been the word used in the Hogarth period). We spent the day working together, and I saw him again the following week in New York, after a performance of the *St. John Passion* in which Hindemith had played the viola d'amore part.

*   *   *

7 Cornelia Street,
New York 14, N.Y.,
22nd November 1948

Dear Igor Stravinsky,

I got back from Washington yesterday afternoon to find your letter. I enclose another verse which should, I think, come first. It is difficult in this metre to get an *exact* rhythmical identity—e.g., *who cares what* is slightly different from *far too soon*, but they are, I hope, near enough. In case you can't read my pencil on the score, here is the verse in printed CAPS:

SOON DAWN WILL GLITTER OUTSIDE THE SHUTTER
AND SMALL BIRDS TWITTER; BUT WHAT OF THAT?
SO LONG AS WE'RE ABLE AND WINE'S ON THE TABLE
WHO CARES WHAT THE TROUBLING DAY IS AT?

I'm very excited about what I hear of the music from Robert Craft. Very Mozartian, he says.

Yours ever,
WYSTAN AUDEN

Three Operas

Via Santa Lucia 22,
Forio d'Ischia,
Prov. di Napoli,
28th April 1949

The sirocco is blowing, which makes it a good day to write letters. Arrived after a *very* boring voyage just before Easter, when the Madonna ran down the street to meet her son, to the sound of explosions. Your photo is up in the kitchen. Hope that Act II is going well. I keep nagging at St. Restituta about it.

Love to all,

WYSTAN

7 Cornelia Street,
New York 14, N.Y.,
24th October 1949

Dear Igor,

Many thanks for your letter.

In order to distinguish Baba in character and emotion from the two lovers, it seems to me that her rhythm should be more irregular and her tempo of utterance faster. In writing her part therefore I have given any line of Baba's twice the number of accents as compared with the equivalent line of Anne's or Tom's. If you find I have given her too many lines, cuts are easy to make.

Much love to you and Vera, and come East soon.

WYSTAN

Three Operas

7 Cornelia Street,
New York 14, N.Y.,
15th November 1949

Dear Igor,

If you haven't yet composed the Trio in Act II, Scene 2, here is an alternative version of Baba's part where the rhymes fit the others, which you may prefer to what I sent you.[1]

Looking forward to hearing *Persephone* on Monday,[2]

Love to you both,

WYSTAN

BABA

I'm waiting, dear. . . . Have done
With talk, my love. . . . I shall count up to ten . . .
Who is she? *One* . . .
Hussy! . . . If I am found
Immured here, dead,
I swear . . . *Two* . . . I'll haunt you . . .
Three . . . You know you're bound
By law, dear . . . *Four* . . . Before I wed
Could I . . . *Five, Six* . . . have . . . *Seven* . . . then
Foreseen my sorrow? . . . *Eight, Nine . . . Ten* . . .
O never, never, never . . .
I shall be cross, love, if you keep
Baba condemned to gasp and weep
Forever.

*   *   *

[1] In fact, the original was kept.
[2] A concert conducted by Robert Craft in Carnegie Hall, in which Auden read a group of his poems.

164

Three Operas

7 *Cornelia Street*,
New York 14, N.Y.,
14th February 1951

Dear Igor,

Many thanks for your letter.

Delighted to hear that Act III, Scene 3, is nearly finished.

Mr. Kallman and I are a bit worried about the directing.[1] As you can imagine, we—as librettists—are as concerned about the stage goings-on as you are about the singing.

If it can possibly be arranged, Kallman and I would like to be present in an advisory capacity when rehearsals start.

Hope you have a lovely time in Cuba.

Love to all,
WYSTAN

Via Santa Lucia 14,
Forio d'Ischia,
Prov. di Napoli,
9th June 1951

Dear Igor,

Thank you for your letter of April. Everything still seems in a terrible muddle here and I hope that we aren't going to have a scratch performance with last-minute singers, designers, etc.

Mr. Kallman, who has been proof-reading the vocal score in New York, writes me that in Act II, Scene 1 (p. 85), stage directions prior to no. 48, the stage direction now indicates that the broadsheet of Baba should be visible to the audience —the face, that is. Did you mean this, because there seem to be two serious objections:

---

[1] It had been settled that the *Rake* was to be produced at La Fenice, Venice, in September.

(1) It is physically impossible to show the broadsheet in such a way that it is equally visible in all parts of the house. Those of the audience who can't see it will be irritated.

(2) More importantly, the revelation that Baba has a beard at this point will ruin the dramatic effect of the finale to Act II, Scene 2.

I know you must be frightfully busy, so don't bother to answer this, unless you violently disagree.

Looking forward to seeing you in Italy,

Love to all,
WYSTAN

[*Florence, October 1958*
Kyoto, April 1959]

APPENDIX

First Scenario for *The Rake's Progress* by Stravinsky and Auden

Place	Characters	Action	Number
ACT I, Sc. 1 Garden of Uncle's Cottage in the country.	Hero and Girl seated.	Pastoral, comme Theocritus, of love, youth, country, etc. (Perhaps mention Adonis here?)	Duet, ten. & sop.
	Uncle appears in doorway.	Blesses (to himself) the pair and looks forward to their marriage.	Trio, ten., sop., bass.
Fine spring afternoon.	Girl & Uncle enter cottage, leaving Hero solus.	Uncle summons Girl into house.	Piano recit.
		Hero walks about garden, humming melody of duo. His voice trails off into silence. Pause. He yawns.	
		Hero turns around. An exchange of questions and enigmatic answers.	Orch. recit., ten. & bass.
	Villain appears at garden gate. He whistles.	Villain explains how his coach has stuck in mid. of lane. Uncle invites him in. Girl goes to fetch wine. They drink. Villain proposes toast to the Future and says he can foretell it. Girl asks him to tell hers.	Piano recit.
	Uncle and Girl reappear from house.	He does so in the manner of a Baroque Delphic Oracle. Egged on by girl, reluctant Hero asks his future.	Bass aria with soli comments.
		A brief silence. Villain whistles. (Villain: 'Read it.')	

167

Place	*Characters*	*Action*	*Number*
ACT I, SC. 1 (continued)	Servant enters with Letter for Hero.	Hero reads Letter announcing illness of Father. 'I must get to London.' Villain offers services.	Orch. recit., ten.
	Curtain	Ensemble in which Hero speaks of Father, Villain of inheritance, Girl and Uncle with foreboding of Future.	Quartet. sop., ten., bass, and bass.
		Orchestral Interlude?	
ACT I, SC. 2 A Brothel. One table with two chairs. Center backstage a grandfather cuckoo clock with an inscription, TEMPUS FUGIT.	Madam, Whores, and Roaring Boys. Enter Hero & Villain. Greeted with great deference by Madam, who escorts them to table.	They sing of the Love of War and the War of Love.	Chorus. Marche Militaire.
		Villain: 'Ne vous dérangez pas, mes amis. Amusez-vous. Dansez.' Hero: 'I want to go home. It is late.' Villain: 'Late? That is easy to change.' (Clock cries One. Clock cries Twelve.) They dance.	Piano recit.
		Villain to Hero: 'Let Madam see if you know your lesson.' He takes him through Catechism of Pleasure.	Gigue. Duet, ten. & bass. Comments by contralto.
		'Now you are ready for confirmation. Your attention, Ladies and Gentlemen.' Villain introduces Hero as Virgin and rich.	Orch. recit.
		Hero sings Serenade of the conventional gallant.	Ten. aria.

Place	Characters	Action	Number
ACT I, SC. 2 (continued)		All applaud and make a rush for Hero. Madam: 'Va-t'en. Ce gosse est à moi.' She leads Hero slowly out, singing him a nursery rhyme. Villain whistles.	*Bruits choriques.* Contralto aria.
	Curtain		
ACT I, SC. 3 Same as SC. 1. Winter Night. Full moon.	Girl comes out of house dressed in traveling clothes.	She speaks of getting no letters, fears Hero has forgotten her and announces her intention to run away from home to London to find him.	Orch. recit. & sop. aria.
ACT II, SC. 1 Hero's dining-room.	Hero en déshabillé at breakfast.	Hero speaks of his debts, his boredom with the bachelor life he has been leading and wonders what to do next. He yawns.	Orch. recit. & ten. aria.
Morning.	Enter Villain whistling.	Villain: 'I have a present for you.' He produces a miniature. Hero: 'Who is this Medusa?' Villain: 'Your wife-to-be.' Hero: 'I'd rather marry a hedgehog.' Villain: 'You will change your mind when I tell you who she is.' He gives a list of her titles.	Piano recit.
		Hero: 'Let me look again. No, I don't think I could.' Villain: 'You know nothing about Marriage. Let me tell you, while you dress.'	Orch. recit. Piano recit.

Place	Characters	Action	Number
ACT II, Sc. 1 (continued)		Gives a lesson in the choice of a wife. Hero gets more and more excited, and joins in.	Bass aria, turning into ten. & bass duet.
	Curtain	When he is ready, Villain cries, 'To Hymen's altar.' Exeunt with bravura.	
ACT II, Sc. 2 Street outside Hero's front door.	Enter Girl. Footman at door.	She expresses her fear at her daring at being alone in the city. She knocks at door. Footman tells her Hero is not at home but expected soon. She comes downstage to a corner.	Orch. sop. recit. Piano recit. sop.
Dusk.	Procession of tradesmen.	Procession of tradesmen arrive with packages. She wonders fearfully what it means, and expresses her love.	Sop. aria.
	Hero and Ugly Duchess in sedan chair. Servants with torches.	Hero and Ugly Duchess arrive.	Marche comique.
	Girl, Hero, Ugly Duchess.	With a cry the Girl rushes forward, confronts Hero, and the fight is on. Girl: 'False one, what of your vows to me?' Hero: 'Let me explain. What shall I say?' Ugly Duchess: 'Who is this person?'	Trio—sop., mezzo & ten.
	Curtain		
ACT II, Sc. 3 (same as Sc. 1)	Hero and Ugly Duchess at breakfast.	Wife chatters about nothing; Hero answers with absent-minded grunts. Wife complains that he doesn't listen or care for her and bursts into hysterics.	Mezzo aria with tenor monosyllables.

Place	Characters	Action	Numbers
Act II, Sc. 3 (continued)		Hero gets up and puts tea-cosy over her head. Sudden silence. He returns to his chair. He yawns.	
	Villain enters. Whistling.	Enter Villain wheeling fantastic apparatus, for making gold out of sea water.	Piano recit.
		Hero: 'What on earth is that?'	
		Villain: 'Your fortune. Watch.' Villain pours water into machine and turns handle, explaining process. A nugget of gold drops out. He hands it to Hero. 'There you are.'	Comic orch. recit.
		He begins to suggest what can be done with absolute wealth. Hero joins in.	Ten. & bass duet.
		Villain: 'Well, will you go into business with me?'	Piano recit.
		Hero: 'Yes.' They shake hands.	
		Villain: 'Will you tell your wife?'	
		Hero: 'It's not necessary.' (Points to her.) 'I have buried her.' They exit with machine.	
	Curtain	Orchestral Interlude	

171

Place	Characters	Action	Number
ACT II, Sc. 4 (Same as previous scene, except that furniture, etc., is stacked as for an auction & covered with cobwebs. Ugly Duchess has not moved.) Afternoon.	Chorus of respectable citizens come to bid.	Chorus sing a moral, while they examine the things.	Chorus.
	Girl.	Enter Girl who runs from one group to another asking for news of Hero. They reply, 'He has disappeared, he ruined himself in a speculation, etc.'	Mezzo & chorus en chuchotant.
	Auctioneer & assts.	Auctioneer enters, mounts dais, starts selling lots of fantastic objects.	Ten. aria.
		Voices in Chorus bid: Lot I Lot II	Chorus bids.
		Lot III is the Ugly Duchess herself, labelled Chose inconnue. Auctioneer plucks tea-cosy off her head. She recognizes Girl and breaks into a tirade, blaming her for everything because Hero only loved her.	Mezzo aria leading to mezzo and sop. duet.
	Hero and Villain off-stage.	Hero & Villain are heard off, singing a street cry—Old Wives for Sale. Ugly Duchess (to Girl): 'Go to him if you want him, I don't.' Girl runs out. Chorus: Quelle histoire.	Ten. & bass in unison. Ensemble.
	Curtain	Orchestral Prelude	

Place	Characters	Action	Numbers
ACT III, Sc. 1 A cemetery. Starless night.	Hero & Villain playing dice on a grave.	Hero: 'Je m'ennuie.' Villain: 'Qu'est-ce que vous désirez maintenant? Le plaisir?' Hero: 'Non.'	Orch. recit.
		Villain: 'La gloire?' Hero: 'Non.' Villain: 'La puissance?' Hero: 'Non.'	
		Villain: 'Quoi donc?' Hero: 'Le passé.' Hero sings of lost innocence and love. Villain: 'Joue, alors.' They play. Hero loses.	Ten. aria.
	Girl (off).	Villain: 'Mon vieux, c'est fini.' He whistles. The voice of the girl is heard in the distance, expressing her undying love for Hero.	Sop. aria (off).
		Hero: (in great excitement) 'Non. Il reste encore une chose. Le futur. Joue.' Villain: 'Je refuse.' Hero: 'Vous ne pouvez pas. Je le commande. Joue.' A clock begins to strike twelve.	
		Villain: 'C'est trop tard.' Hero: 'J'arrête le temps. Ecoute.' The clock stops in the middle of its striking.	

173

Place	Characters	Action	Numbers
ACT III, Sc. 1 (continued)		Villain sings with defiant despair of the future of a love that he can never have.	
		Hero: 'Assez. Joue.' They play. Villain loses. Hero: 'Eh bien. Siffle.' Silence. 'Siffle! !' Silence. 'Siffle! ! !'	Orch. recit.
		Villain sinks into the grave. The clock finishes its striking. Hero: 'Let it strike. Le temps ne m'effraye plus. Pour l'amour il n'y a pas de passé ou de futur, il n'y a que le présent. Amant et aimé, je suis l'Adonis, le toujours jeune.'	Bass arioso.
	Curtain		
ACT III, Sc. 2 Bedlam.	Hero. Chorus.	Hero: 'Levez-vous, mes amis, couronnez-vous de fleurs. Vénus, reine de l'amour me visitera.'	Ten. solo & chorus.
		Chorus: 'Elle ne viendra jamais.' Hero: 'Elle m'a fait sa promesse.' Chorus: 'Elle ne la tiendra pas.'	
	Hero and Chorus of Madmen.	They dance, mocking him. Hero sinks his face in his hands.	Danse choquante.

174

Place	Characters	Action	Numbers
ACT III, Sc. 2 (continued)	Enter Keeper and Girl.	Keeper (to Chorus): 'Allez-vous en.' (Chorus retire.) (to Girl): 'Le voilà. N'ayez pas peur. Il n'est pas dangereux. Seulement, il s'imagine l'Adonis. Entrez dans son jeu et il sera satisfait.'	Piano recit.
	Exit Keeper.	Girl: s'approche du Hero et l'appelle par son nom. Il léve la tête.	
		Hero: 'At last, Venus, tu es arrivée. Je t'ai attendue si longtemps. Ces types là m'ont dit que tu m'as oublié. Monte à ton trône.' (He leads her to his chair and kneels at her feet.)	Orch recit., ten.
		'O Vénus, ma vraie déesse, pardonne-moi mes péchés. J'ai dedaigné ton amour en chassant les ombres stupides. Mais maintenant le sanglier est mort et tout est changé. Je sais que je t'aime comme tu m'aimes. Pardonne-moi, je t'implore.'	Ten. aria, then ten. & sop. duet.
		Girl: 'Si tu m'aimes il n'y a rien à pardonner.'	
		Both: 'L'amour change—chaque enfer particulier a l'Elysée mutuelle.'	
		Hero: 'Laisse-moi placer ma tête à tes genoux. Je suis fatigué et je veux dormir. Chante, Vénus, chante à ton enfant.'	Orch. recit.
		Girl sings a lullaby. Hero falls asleep.	Sop. aria.
	Enter Keeper with Uncle.	Uncle (to Girl, tout simplement): 'The tale is ended. I have come to take you home.'	Piano recit.

175

Place	Characters	Action	Numbers
ACT III, Sc. 2 (continued)			
	Exeunt Keeper, Uncle & Girl.	Girl (to Hero, aussi très simplement): 'Adieu. Dors tranquillement.' Le héros s'éveille brusquement.	Orch. recit.
		Hero: 'Où es-tu, Vénus? Où es-tu? Les oiseaux chantent, les fleurs s'ouvrent. C'est le printemps. Viens. Vite. Je veux coucher avec toi.' 'Holà Achille, Hélène, Orphée, Platon, Eurydice, Perséphone. Où est ma Vénus? Vous l'avez volée pendant que je dormais. Où l'avez vous cachée?'	
	Re-enter Chorus.	Chorus: 'Il n'y avait personne ici.' Hero: 'Mon coeur se brise. La mort approche. Pleurez, mes amis, pleurez pour moi, l'Adonis le toujours jeune, l'Adonis que Vénus a aimé.' Chorus: 'Nous pleurons pour Adonis, le jeune, le beau, que Vénus a aimé.'	Fugal chorus.
	Curtain		
Epilogue	Before the Curtain.	Hero, Girl, Villain, Wife and Uncle sing a moral, THE DEVIL FINDS WORK FOR IDLE HANDS TO DO.	Quintet.

FIN

176

INDEX

(*Note:* S. indicates Stravinsky)

Accompaniment to a Cinematographic Scene (Schoenberg), 108
Ad Dominum cum Tribularer (Hassler), 116
Agnus Dei (Josquin), 107
Alexander III, Emperor, 25
Alexander Park, St. Petersburg, 23
Alexandra, Queen of England, 86
Alexandro-Nevsky cemetery, 21
Alfonso XIII, 43, 86
Alma Nemes (Lasso), 116
Altenberg Lieder (Berg), 122, 122n
Amériques (Varèse), 103
Andersen, Hans, 63
Andreyev (writer), 28
Ansermet, Ernest, 23
Apollo (S.), 43
Après-midi d'un Faune (Debussy), 36, 39
Arcana (Varèse), 103
Arensky, Anton, 61–2
Aristophanes, 155
'Arrow' scores, 124, 124n
Auden, W. H., 145, 154–76
Au-dessus de la mêlée (Rolland), 78
Auer's violin school, 18
Autobiography (S.), 131, 144
Ave Maria (S.), 152n

Baba Yaga (Liadov), 63
Babbitt, Milton, 120–1
Bach, J. S., 23, 23n, 29, 39, 111, 117, 121, 134, 140
Baiser de la Fée (S.), 35, 45
Bakst, 146
Balalaika in *Pièces Faciles* (S.), 99
Balanchine, George, 33, 37, 43, 69
Balmont, Konstantin, 66, 82, 83
Bashō and Busōn haiku, 150
Baude Cordier, 107
Beecham, Sir Thomas, 83, 133, 133n
Beethoven, 23, 23n, 74, 75, 111, 112, 112n, 140
Beethoven the Creator (Rolland), 80
Belayev, 29, 59
Benois, Alexander, 32, 132, 133, 134–43
Benois, Anna Karlovna, 141
Berceuses du Chat (S.), 98
Berg, 56, 103, 104, 110
Berio, 101
Berlin Radio Orchestra, 152
Berne Copyright Convention, 96n
Berners, Lord (formerly G. Tyrwhitt), 83–5
'Bertha', S.'s childhood nurse, 20
Blavatsky, Madame, 66
Blok, Alexander, 83
Blumenfeld, Felix, 59

Index

Bohlen, Charles, 22
Bolm, Adolphe, 43
Borodin, 20, 98
Boston Symphony Orchestra, 99
Boulez, 123, 125
Brahms, 23, 28, 29, 110, 123
Bruckner, 29
Busch, Wilhelm, 34

Calmo, 116
Capriccio (S.), 97n
Capriccio Espagnol (Rimsky-Korsakov), 58
Cardano, 114
Carmen Sylva, Queen of Rumania, 87
Carnegie Hall, 164n
Carol, King of Rumania, 87
Catherine the Great, 17
Cecchetti, Enrico, 33, 34
Cecchetti, Signora, 33
Chant Funèbre for Rimsky-Korsakov (S.), 54, 59
Chaplin, Charles, 109
Char, René, 127
Chicago Art Institute, 154
Chinoiserie (Tyrwhitt), 85
Choral Preludes (Bach), 117
Chout (Prokofiev ballet), 69
'Chromatic Duo' (Willaert), 116n
Cingria, Charles-Albert, 19
Cinq Pièces Faciles (S.), 95, 99
Claudel, 80, 152
Clemens non Papa, 116
Cocteau, 45
Coleridge, S. T., 115
Così fan Tutti (Mozart), 158
Couperin, 29
Craft, Robert, 162, 164n
Credo (S), 152n
Cui, César, 60–1, 98
Cunard, Lady, 85
Cyprus Codex, 107

Dalcroze, 52, 52n
d'Annunzio, G., 146
Dargomizhsky, 61

Debussy, 28, 49, 59, 65, 81, 131n, 132, 133, 144, 145
Delage, Maurice, 96
Delius, Frederick, 133n
Density 21.5 (Varèse), 103
Deplus (clarinettist), 111
Descartes, 78
Diaghilev, 17, 21, 32, 33, 34, 35, 36, 38, 39, 40, 41, 41–2n, 43–53, 64, 65, 66, 69, 81, 83, 85, 86, 92, 93, 96, 101–2, 109, 131, 132, 133, 135n, 141
Dickens, 28
Dieu Bleu (Hahn), 81
Don Giovanni (Mozart), 91
Dostoievsky, 21, 27, 38, 142
Doubles (Boulez), 125
'Down St. Peter's Road' (song in *Petroushka*, (S.)), 97
Dream on the Volga (Arensky), 61–2
Dubuffet, 41
Dukas, 28
Dumbarton Oaks Concerto (S.), 77

Eccentric (S.), 95
Eliot, T. S., 162
Epitaphium (S.), 105
Erlanger, Baroness Catherine d', 159, 159n
Eroica Symphony, 23
Esterházy family, 91, 93
Etudes, Op. 7 (S.), 65
'Evenings of Contemporary Music', St. Petersburg Concert series, 28, 29, 66
Everardi, Professor, 18
Excelsior (Paris paper), 76

Falla, Manuel de, 46, 80–1
Faune et la Bergère, Le (S.), 29, 59
Félicité (Flaubert), 159n
Fenice, La (Venice), 165n
Firebird, The (S.), 32, 33, 34, 35, 43, 55, 59, 61, 62, 63, 65, 86, 96n, 98
Fireworks (S.), 32, 56
Five Pieces for Orchestra (Schoenberg), 122

Index

Flaubert, 159n
F minor Fantasia (Schubert), 64
Fokine, 32, 33–5, 41, 43, 48, 69
Ford Foundation, 93
Four Norwegian Moods (S.), 108
Four Russian Peasant Choruses (S.), 98
Four Russian Songs (S.), 98
Freud, 114
Funeral Music for Queen Mary (Purcell), 106
Furman, Roman, 17
Futurism, 66, 101, 102

Gagliano, Marco da, 116
Gazzelloni (flute player), 111
Gesualdo, 116, 117
Gide, André, 74, 75, 77, 144–53
Glazunov, 29, 29n, 34, 55n, 59
Godebski, Cipa, 80
Gogol, 21, 142
Goldoni, 141
Golovine, 136n
Good Earth, The (film version), 108
Gorky, 28
Gorodetsky, S., 82, 83
Gorodetsky songs (S.), 28, 48, 82–3
Gourévitch Gymnasium, 26–7
Greeting Prelude (S.), 97
Greiter, Matthias, 116
Grieg, 99
Grigoriev, 39, 39n
Groddeck, 158
Gruppen (Stockhausen), 118, 119, 120, 125

Hahn, Reynaldo, 81–2
Hamlet, 91, 101
Hamsun, 28
Hansel and Gretel, 132
'Happy Birthday' melody in *Greeting Prelude* (S.), 97
Hassler, Hans Leo, 116
Hauptmann, Gerhardt, 28
Haydn, 91, 110, 112, 113
Hindemith, 110, 122, 123, 152, 162
Histoire du Soldat, L' (S.), 43–4, 122

Hoffmann, 33, 34, 63
Hogarth, 154, 162
Hugo, Victor, 152
Huizinga, 117
Humplik, Josef, 103
Huxley, Aldous, 56, 154
Huysmans, 65

Ibsen, 28
Idzikovsky, 42
Ielatchitch, Alexander, 22, 23, 58
Imperial Symphony Orchestra, and Theatre, St. Petersburg, 29, 35, 36
d'Indy, 28, 28n, 29
Intégrales (Varèse), 103
Ionisation (Varèse), 103
Ivanhoe (Scott), 28
Ives, Charles, 118
Izvolsky, Ambassador, 36

'Jambe en bois' melody in *Petroushka* (S.), 96, 97
Janacopulos, Vera, 69
Japanese Lyrics (Ravel), 70
Jaroslav, 22
Jean-Christophe (Rolland), 80, 80n
Jemchooshnikov brothers, 142n, 143
Jeux (Debussy), 39, 122, 122n
Johnson, Dr., 44
Jone, Hildegarde, 103
Josephslegende (*Joseph and Potiphar*) (Strauss), 39, 39n, 42
Josquin, 107
Joyce, James, 78

Kallman, Chester, 160, 160n, 165
Kanjincho play (Kabuki Theatre), 150n
Karsavina, 24, 43
Kasatchov (Tyrwhitt), 85
Kashperova, Mlle, 25–6
Kholodovsky, Kiril, 18
Kholodovsky, Sophie, 22
'Khorovode themes' of *Firebird* (S.), 98
Khvotschinsky, 52
Kikimora (Liadov), 63

Index

Klee, Paul, 78
Kleines harmonisches Labyrinth (Bach?), 117
Klukovsky, 83
Krenek, 110
Kronstadt, 19
Kuramatengu (Noh play), 121
Kussevitsky, 30, 48, 49, 139, 140

Lägerlof, Selma, 28
Larionov, Michael, 109
Lasso, 116
League of Composers, 94
Legend of Joseph (ballet, R. Strauss), see *Josephslegende*
Leskov, 21
Liadov, Anatol, 62–4, 66, 97
Lifar, 43
Life for the Tsar, A, 31
Liszt, 64
'Little Tich', 95
Liturgie (proposed ballet, S.), 48, 48n, 101
Lopokova, 43
Lowinsky, Professor, 116, 116n
Luste (Valéry), 77
Luzzaschi, 116

Maeterlinck, M., 63
Mahler, G., 57, 58
Malatesta, Sigismondo, 94, 95
Mallarmé, 69
Mann, Klaus, 99
Mardzhanov, 136, 141
Maria, Queen of Rumania, 86–7
Maria, Queen of Spain, 86
Mariinsky Theatre, St. Petersburg, 68
Marinetti, 102
Marteau sans Maître, Le (Boulez), 123
Martyre de S. Sébastien (Debussy), 145–6
Massine, 38, 42–3, 44, 50
Mavra (S.), 81
Medici, Giovanni di, 94
Merezhkovsky, 83
Messiaen, 110

Mestrovic, 48, 48n, 50
Meyerhold, 136n
Miakovsky, 67
Michelangelo's *Conversion of St. Paul*, 41
Mironov, 55
Mirsky, Prince, 83
Mitusov, Stepan, 29, 97, 136, 136n
'Monday Evening Concerts' (Los Angeles), 29
Monsieur Teste (Valéry), 74
Montéclair, 29
Monteux, Pierre, 97, 132, 144–5
Monteverdi, 29
Moore, G. E., 114
Morges, 20
Moscow Conservatory, 62
Movements for piano and orchestra (S.), 106–7
Mozart, 23, 111, 112, 118, 125
Mozart and Salieri (Rimsky-Korsakov), 57
Musical Snuff Box (Liadov), 63
Mussorgsky, 132, 133
My Faust (Valéry), 77, 78
Mystères de New York, Les (film), 109

Napravnik (conductor), 24
Natashka (S.), 70
Nicolaevitch, Alexander, 65
Nicolson, Sir Harold, 86
Nightingale, The (S.), 42, 43, 51, 85, 131–43
Night Train (film), 154
Nijinska, Bronislava, 40, 41
Nijinsky, 33, 34, 35–41, 42, 43, 48, 50, 50n, 135, 135n
Noces, Les (S.), 40, 43, 48, 48n, 50, 51, 67, 97, 100, 101, 102, 122
Notturno (Mozart), 124
Norton Lectures, Harvard, 74
Norwegian Moods (S.), 99
Nossenko, Catherine, see Stravinsky, Catherine
Notes on Chopin (Gide), 75
Nouvel, Walter, 46–7, 66, 134n

180

Index

Novodevitchy cemetery, St. Petersburg, 21

Octandre (Varèse), 103
Odyssey of Homer, 147
Omaggio à Joyce (Berio), 101
Only One, The (Valéry), 77, 78
Oresteia, The (Taneyev), 62
Orff, 123
Orwell, G., 40
Ostrovsky (librettist), 57
Oustiloug, 60, 132n

Passacaglia (*Altenberg Lieder*), 122n
Pastorale (S.), 56n
Pater Noster (S.), 152, 152n
Pavlova, 32, 43
Pavlovka, estate of A. Ielatchitch, 22
People and Things (Nicolson), 86
Pergolesi, 92
Petipa (choreographer), 31
Persephone (S. and Gide), 74, 75, 76, 144–52, 164, 164n
Petrenko, Miss (singer), 28
Petroushka (S.), 33, 34, 38, 40, 41, 43, 55, 65, 67, 80, 95, 96, 96n, 97n, 132, 133n
Petrovna, Evgenia (S.'s housekeeper), 159, 159n
Picasso, 84
Pierrot Lunaire (Schoenberg), 95, 122
Piltz, Mlle, 37, 43
Poetics of Music (S., Harvard lectures), 74
Poets of Russia 1890–1930 (Renato Poggioli), 82n
Pokrovsky, Ivan, 29
Polignac, Princess Edmond de, 73, 80
Ponti, Carlo, 85
Pound, Ezra, 95
Pratella, 102
Pribaoutki (S.), 69, 98
Prince Igor (Borodin), 34
Prokofiev, 48, 51, 64, 66–70, 102
Prootkov, Kosma, 142, 142n
Proust, 81

Pulcinella (S.), 42, 81, 92
Purcell, 84, 104, 116, 117, 145
Pushkin, 57, 152

Quid Non Ebrietas quartet (Willaert), 116

Rachmaninov, 21
Ragtime (S.), 85
Rake's Progress (S.), 94, 145, 154–76
Ramuz, C. F. 74, 80, 152
Rasputin, 28
Ravel, 28, 43, 65, 74, 81, 132, 144
Rayleigh, Lord (*Theory of Sound*), 114
Reger, 28
Renard (S.), 23, 40, 41n, 43, 44, 67, 97, 102n, 142n
Retablo de Maese Pedro, El (Falla), 80
Richter, Nicolas, 28
Ricordi, 51
Rilke, 80n
Rimsky-Korsakov, 18, 20, 21, 22, 27, 29, 54–60, 61, 62, 63, 64, 66, 97, 140
Rimsky-Korsakov, Andrei, 20–1, 55
Rimsky-Korsakov, Michael, 20
Rimsky-Korsakov, Nadezhda, 56, 56n
Rimsky-Korsakov, Sophia, 56
Rimsky-Korsakov, Vladimir, 22, 55–6, 140
Ripon, Lady, 36–7, 86
Rockefeller Foundation, 93
Roerich, 133, 134
Rolland, Romain, 78–80, 80n
Romains, Jules, 80
Romanov, Boris, 132
Roosevelt, Mrs. F. D., 99
Rore, 116
Rossetti, Stefano, 116
Rossini, 111
Rubinstein, Anton, 64
Rubinstein, Ida, 34–5, 46, 145, 146, 147, 148, 149, 150
Russalka (Dargomizhsky), 61
Russell, Henry, 51

Index

Russian Dance, from *Petroushka* (S.), 96

'Russian Symphony Concerts', Belayev's, 29, 59

Russo-Japanese War, 27

Rybinsk, 22

Sacre du Printemps, (S.), 23, 28n, 36, 37, 38, 39, 42, 43, 65, 66–7, 81, 96n, 98, 103, 115, 122, 122n, 131, 131n, 139, 140, 141, 144, 145

Sadko (Rimsky-Korsakov), 59, 59n

St. John Passion (Bach), 162

St. Petersburg Conservatory, 18, 21, 63

St. Petersburg Gymnasium, 26

St. Petersburg Military Institute, 60

St. Petersburg University, 27–8, 46

Salomon series of Symphonies (Haydn), 112

Samara estate (A. Ielatchitch), 22

San Francisco 'Vortex' experiment, 101

Sanin, Alexander, 132, 141

San Martino, President (of the Santa Cecilia), 49, 51

Santayana, George, 158

Scherzo à la Russe (S.), 108

Scherzo Fantastique (S.), 32, 61

Schoenberg, 92, 95, 97n, 108, 114, 122, 122n

Schubert, 25, 64

Schumann, 25

Schütz, 118

Scott, Sir Walter, 28

Scriabin, 63, 64–6

Semiramis (Valéry), 76

Serenade (Schoenberg), 122

Sert, Misia, 74, 144, 146

Sessions, 110

Shaw, G. B., 77

Skorohodova, Alexandra Ivanovna, 13, 18

Sleeping Beauty, The (Tchaikovsky), 31

Snow Maiden, The (Rimsky-Korsakov), 57, 60

Sokolov, Mme, 159, 159n

Sokolova, 43

Soulima-Stravinsky family, 17

Spalding, Albert, 96n

Spencer, Mr. (of 'Jambe en Bois' song), 96

Star-spangled Banner (S. arranges), 99, 100

Steinberg, M., 21, 56

Stockhausen, 117, 118, 119, 120, 125

Stone Guest, The (Dargomizhsky), 61

Strauss, Richard, 39, 42, 49

Stravinsky, Anna Kholodovsky (S.'s mother), 13, 24

Stravinsky, Catherine Nossenko (S.'s first wife), 13, 18, 134, 136, 139, 141

Stravinsky, Feodor Ignatievitch (S.'s father), 13, 18, 19–20, 24, 31

Stravinsky, Goury (S.'s brother), 13 20, 21, 24, 52, 58; Roman (S.'s brother), 13, 20, 21; Youry (S.'s brother), 13, 20, 21

Stravinsky, Ludmila (S.'s elder daughter), 13, 18; Maria Milena (S.'s younger daughter), 139, 139n

Stravinsky, Tatiana (Youry's daughter), 20

Stravinsky, Vera (S.'s wife), 68, 82, 84, 159, 160, 163

Strindberg, A., 28

Südermann, 28

Suhodolsky, 141

Suite, Op. 29 (Schoenberg), 103

Svetlov, 135

Symbolism, 66, 101

Symphony in A major (Mozart), 112

Symphony, Beethoven's Second, 112

Symphony in E flat (S.), 58

Symphony of Psalms (S.), 81, 97n

Symphony in Three Movements (S.), 23

Symphony (Webern) commissioned by League of Composers, 94

Index

Symphonies of Wind Instruments (S.), 97n, 122

Taneyev, Serge, 62, 64
Tartakov, 21
Tavern Keeper, The (Goldoni), 141
Tchaikovsky, 21, 28, 55, 57, 58, 61, 62, 97, 98
Tchekov, 109
Tcherepnine, 68
Tchernicheva, 43
Teliakovsky, Director of St. Petersburg Opera, 51
Theory of Sound (Rayleigh), 114
Thomas à Kempis, 115
Three Pieces for String Quartet (S.), 95
Thurn und Taxis, Princess M. von, 80n
Tocqueville, A. de, 158
Tolstoy, 44n, 142n, 143, 151
Tolstoy, Countess, 62
Toscanini, 111, 112, 132
Tricorne, Le (Falla), 81
Triumph of Neptune (Tyrwhitt), 83
Tsar Saltan (Rimsky-Korsakov), 22
Twain, Mark, 28
Tyrwhitt, Gerald, 83–5

Uncle Armand (song, S.), 69, 70

Valéry, Paul, 73–8, 152
Valse (in S.'s Second Suite for Small Orchestra), 63
Valse Sentimentale (Tyrwhitt), 85
Varèse, Edgar, 102–3

Variations for Orchestra (Webern), 120, 125
Variations on a Theme by Haydn (Brahms), 110
Varlich (Imperial Kapellmeister), 59
Vassili, Diaghilev's servant, 45
Verlaine, Paul, 21, 41
Villiers de l' Isle Adam, P.A., 65
Vincentino, 121
Voyage au Congo (Gide), 151

Wagner, 60, 61, 116, 124, 140
Waiting for Godot (Beckett), 77
Waldmüller portrait of Beethoven, 23
Weber, 34
Webern, 78, 94, 95, 103–6, 109, 110, 120, 122, 122n, 123, 125
Wedding Bouquet (Tyrwhitt), 83
Wert, 116
Whiteman, Paul, 108
Wihtol, Joseph, 63
Willaert, 116, 121
Williams, Charles, 157–8
Wolkonsky, Prince, 35–6
Woolf (teacher of mathematics to S.), 27
Wozzeck (Berg), 122

Yeats, W. B., 158
Yussupov, Nicolai, 27

Zarlino, 121
Zeitmasse (Stockhausen), 118
Zvezdoliki (Balmont), 83
Zyklus (Stockhausen), 118